TELEVISION
and the Fear
of Crime

TELEVISION and the Fear of Crime

Barrie Gunter

Senior Research Officer
Independent Broadcasting Authority

British Library Cataloguing in Publication Data
Gunter, Barrie
    Television and the fear of crime. — (Television
    research monograph, ISSN 0951-3582;2)
    1. Violence in television — social aspects
    I. Title   II. Series
    302.2'345   HM258

    ISBN 0-86196-118-8
    ISBN 0-86196-119-6 Pbk

Published by
John Libbey & Company Ltd
80/84 Bondway, London SW8 1SF, England (01) 582 5266
John Libbey Eurotext Ltd
6 rue Blanche, 92120 Montrouge, France (1) 47 35 85 52

Typesetting in Century by E E Owens & Co Ltd., London SE15 4AZ
Printed in Great Britain by Whitstable Litho Ltd, Whitstable, Kent

Contents

Chapter 1

Concern about crime

Each year reports on the latest official crime statistics presented in the press and on broadcast news programmes paint a picture of an increasingly dangerous world ridden with crime and violence, in which any of us could, with increased likelihood, find ourselves falling prey. But what is the public's experience of crime? How concerned are people today about being victimised? And what is the role of television, in comparison with direct experience and other sources of influence, in cultivating public beliefs about and fears of crime?

This monograph is concerned principally with the last question. The ensuing discussion has grown out of a broader debate about the depiction of violence on television and the influence this has on viewers. While much of the controversy surrounding the showing of violence on television, both in the news and on drama programming designed for audience entertainment, has centred most often on the supposed stimulation such portrayals might provide causing the increased occurrence of violence in real life, there has more recently developed concern that frequent watching of crime-related content on the box encourages people to become more afraid to venture out, believing that if they do they will fall victim to criminal elements waiting outside to get them. Research evidence from the United States has been presented in support of the view that regular viewing of television drama (which through independent descriptive content analyses is identified as containing a great deal of violence) is connected with exaggerated public perceptions of the incidence of violent crime and greater fear of it. Attempts to reproduce this link in Britain, however, has shown that the American findings do not travel well. This monograph will review this evidence, report the latest research done in Britain, and argue that when considered against other social forces and in the context of the way people use and react to programmes, the influence of television on public perceptions and fears of crime is not very strong.

1

Experience of crime

Before looking at the influence of media content on perceptions and fear of crime, it might be useful to consider to what extent people have generally experienced crime themselves and have anxieties about it. To begin with, does public concern about crime depend on the actual incidence of crime - either as it is reported to them or as they actually experience it? Official crime figures point regularly to increases in various crimes. But are these trends reflected also in anxieties people have about personal involvement in crime? Indeed how reliable are the published crime figures?

Traditionally, published crime statistics are derived from reports received by the police. These figures, however, may offer only a poor indication of the extent of crime, and reflect only a part of all the criminal activity which pervades society. The police learn about crime from victims. But there are many occasions when the victim chooses not to report incidents to the police. These 'hidden' crimes nevertheless represent very real experiences for those who are victimised and may colour their perceptions of the world around them.

An alternative perspective on assessing the extent and impact of crime, which takes into account the experiences and perceptions of victims, is the crime survey. Crime surveys have been carried out in a number of countries and typically involve interviews with randomly selected national samples to find out about their personal experiences as victims of selected crimes. This sort of investigation can provide a useful indication of the extent of different crimes and may reveal facts and figures not normally contained in official police statistics. The first British Crime Survey was carried out in 1981 among 11,000 households in England and Wales and another 5,000 in Scotland. A second survey was carried out in England and Wales only in 1984, which provided estimates of various crimes up to the end of 1983. In both cases, respondents were asked if they had been victims of different kinds of crime. Crimes were broken down into *personal* offences (e.g. assaults, robberies, theft from the person, sexual offences) and *household* offences (e.g. car theft, theft from and/or vandalism to property, domestic burglary). A significant new line of enquiry included in this survey was the degree to which respondents were afraid or anxious about crime.

In the most recent British Crime Survey (Hough and Mayhew, 1985), offences against the person involving violence were heavily outweighed by offences involving theft and damage to property. Although it was felt that there may have been certain under-estimations of crimes of violence against the person reported by victims, 1983 figures showed that wounding, robbery, sexual offences and common assaults comprised 17 percent of all offences. Excluding common assaults, the figure dropped to five percent. Half of these offences involved strangers.

One of the most common types of crime was theft from and damage to motor vehicles, which represented nearly one in three of all crimes uncovered by the survey. Overall, the survey revealed a 10 percent increase in crime between 1981 and 1983, which compared favourably with the 12 percent increase recorded in police figures.

There were increases in most areas of crime on which information was obtained in the British Crime Surveys of 1981 and 1983. The most significant increases occurred in household burglary and bicycle theft. Crimes of violence against the person were not substantial. And although the figures indicated an apparently considerable increase in reported sexual offences, the data were regarded as unreliable because of changes to the line of questioning on this subject.

Fear of crime

Fear of crime is a distinct conceptual judgement from perceptions of likelihood of personal victimisation. A person may have a heightened sense of personal risk from crime and yet be totally or relatively unconcerned about it. And yet someone else who believes that their chance of falling victim is remote, may nevertheless be very anxious at the thought that it could happen. There is no doubt that the experience of victimisation is very frightening for most people, and the immediate prospect of falling prey to criminal elements may elicit a powerful fear reaction. According to some researchers, however, perceptions and emotional states are distinct psychological entities (Zillmann and Wakshlag, 1985). Therefore, fear of crime and assessments of risk are not necessarily linked (Garofalo and Laub, 1982). A degree of association between perceptions and fearfulness can exist though, especially where beliefs about crime are grossly exaggerated representations of the facts. It is under these circumstances where media influences are often invoked as having a significant part to play.

Several distinct questions about fear of crime were included in the British Crime Survey. Respondents were asked first of all how safe they felt when walking alone after dark in their own neighbourhood.

In 1983 around one in three (31 percent) said they felt "fairly unsafe" or "very unsafe", a slight decrease on 1981 (34 percent). Generally, women (48 percent) were more likely than men (13 percent) to feel unsafe, with very little change occurring over time. Further questions asked about fears relating to specific types of crime. Men were less worried about being mugged (13 percent) than about being burgled (18 percent), while women were equally worried about both types of crime (27-28 percent). Women generally (30 percent), but expecially young women under 30 (41 percent) were most concerned of all about rape.

People were found, however, to overestimate risks of falling victim to crimes, and this might have contributed to their levels of concern. Women, as we have noted above, were very worried about rape, but tended to hold exaggerated estimates of its likelihood which were far in excess of statistical probability of their being victimised. Degrees of worry about burglary tended to vary depending on area of residence suggesting that people may have some grasp of the relative likelihood of break-ins. However, personal estimates revealed that people in all areas had distorted impressions about personal risk from burglary. Over-estimation of actual risks was highest in areas where burglary was relatively infrequent, with those who over-estimated also expressing the greatest anxiety.

There was evidence that fear of crime restricts people's behaviour. One in two women interviewed said they avoided going out unaccompanied after dark. In high crime areas one person in 25 said they never went out after dark, with fear of victimisation being a major reason. Placed in a broader context of general dissatisfactions and perceived social and environmental problems, however, in most areas crime was outranked by other concerns such as poor amenities and shopping facilities, traffic and poor public transport. Crime emerged as a more serious problem for people who lived in areas of high risk.

Although not an overriding concern of most people, the British Crime Survey did reveal that public beliefs about crime do not invariably reflect actual incidence of crime or risk probabilities. Are such misconceptions produced to any extent by information received through media sources to which members of the public are exposed? According to some writers, the media play a significant role in the cultivation of distorted public conceptions about crime.

Media and crime

Writers on media coverage of crime have for many years been virtually unanimous in their contention that media coverage of crime is biased; there is little or no correspondence between objective characteristics of crime and crime as it is portrayed or reported in the media (Isaacs, 1961; Quinney, 1970; Conklin, 1971). Distortions in the reporting of crime were believed to contribute to misconceptions about the prevalence of different sorts of crime and lead to exaggerated public fear of crime (Conklin, 1975). Some writers observed that the media sometimes were responsible for the artificial production of crime waves. Newspapers would use crime news to build circulation (Bell, 1962). Similarly, changes in police reporting practices might produce apparent shifts in certain crime rates which though little more than statistical artifacts (Cook, 1971), could be played upon by the media to give the impression of an upsurge in actual criminal activity.

Other critics have emphasised the failure of the media to place reports of major crimes in a proper historical or statistical perspective. Prominent coverage of serious violent crimes made sensational copy but could also produce inflated public perceptions of the frequency of what in reality are the least frequent of crimes (Conklin, 1975). Media reports seldom present information on victimisation rates or trends, so that the public, lacking this essential contextual background, are often unintentionally misled by the media to believe that the world is a far more dangerous place than it really is.

Criticisms of the media in their coverage of crime embody concerns that are built on certain fundamental assumptions about the way crime information is presented in the media and about the ways people interact with media content. Several steps can be identified in this process. First, there is the premise that there are inherent distortions in media reporting of crime; second, it is assumed that the media represent an important if not the major source of information about crime; third, media information is accepted largely uncritically by the public; and fourth, the public absorb media misinformation into their existing belief systems unaltered to develop inaccurate conceptions about crime in the real world. In addition to this cognitive effect, there is also an emotional component – that of fear. Distorted beliefs about crime, which generally mean overestimates about the incidence of criminal activity in society, are hypothesised to give rise also to exaggerated anxieties about falling victim to crime.

The cultivation model of TV influence

The concern about the impact of media portrayals of violence and crime-related themes dates back to before the days of television. In the 1920s, coordinated social scientific research was conducted into the portrayal and impact of crime in Hollywood movies. This research, which was funded by a private philanthropic foundation called the Payne Fund, found that crime was one of the major themes in movies but no conclusive evidence emerged that they actually had degenerating effects on their audiences. (Blumer and Hauser, 1933; Dale, 1935, Dysinger and Ruckmick, 1933).

Early research into media influences was dominated by what came to be known as a 'hypodermic model'. The basic theoretical assumption was that media content would produce specific changes in the attitudes and behaviour of those exposed to it. In the context of television violence, for example, researchers investigated whether regular watching of programmes containing violence could produce an increase in aggressive dispositions or antisocial conduct among viewers.

The notion that the mass media can have powerful direct effects on people was seriously challenged, as long as a quarter of a century ago, however (Klapper, 1960). And although media influences on early socialisation have not been entirely dismissed, they are generally regarded as relatively weak influences compared with those of the family, school, peers and real world experiences.

Despite continued attempts by experimental researchers to demonstrate short-term, cause-effect relationships between television and behaviour (Bandura, 1973, 1977; Berkowitz, 1970; Leyens, Camino, Parke and Berkowitz, 1975; Parke, Berkowitz, Leyens, West and Sebastian, 1977; Liebert and Baron, 1972; Tannenbaum and Zillmann, 1975), increasingly today it is believed that the most significant naturally-occurring influences of television may be long-term ones. According to some researchers, television's influence may occur through passive learning (Krugman and Hartley, 1971). In line with this notion is the belief that regular viewing of television, and more especially of its violence-containing programmes, over many years may have a gradual cumulative impact on viewers' perceptions of the world and on their behaviour in it.

This belief is central to the cultivation theory of television's influence introduced by Gerbner and his associates during the early 1970s (Gerbner, 1972; Gerbner and Gross, 1976). Whereas public and scientific debate about television violence was built on the fundamental assumption that television's effects are essentially anti-normative, antisocial and disruptive, this new model conceived of the medium as an instrument of the established socio-cultural and industrial order that serves to maintain and reinforce the political, economic and cultural status quo. The main function of television is enculturation. This socialisation process serves to strengthen rather than to undermine socio-cultural norms. Gerbner and his colleagues have argued that this gradual and cumulative cultivation by television of adherence to the dominant beliefs, values and accepted codes of conduct is far more widespread and significant than are any disruptive consequences of exposure to discrete, antisocial portrayals in programmes.

Television violence is conceptualised as a demonstration of power. Television drama is believed to teach lessons not so much in the way conceived by imitation theorists with regard to how to behave violently, but does so instead through symbolic demonstrations of who in the world has power such as are provided by stereotyped patterns of showing who wins and who loses in the conflicts which characterise so many television storylines. Cumulative exposure to these recurring patterns of portrayed violence and victimisation may result not only in viewers learning about the power structure of the world of television drama, but through a process of generalisation to a television-biased colouration of their outlook on reality. Television provides a symbolic environment which can shape and organise social experience through the system of beliefs and values it conveys. In this sense, television fulfils a function once the province of religion. According to Gerbner and Gross (1976) "The newly universal, non-selective and habitual use of television fits the naturalistic pattern of its programming. You watch television as you might attend a church service, except that most people watch television more religiously" (p.177).

The cultural indicators project

The conceptionalisation of television drama as a symbolic reflection and manifestation of the dominant social and cultural norms has been investigated empirically in a project called Cultural Indicators, where empirical analysis occurs at two levels. The research begins with a coding technique called message system analysis which provides a descriptive account of the content of television drama. The objective of this technique is to identify aspects of the television world whose contribution to viewers' beliefs about the real world can subsequently be tested. The mode of analysis itself does not include subjective judgements about television programmes on the part of viewers. Instead, items and areas of analysis are specified on an *a priori* basis by the researchers themselves, who provide an operational framework for programme assessment which is utilised in an objective fashion by trained coders.

Message system analysis has revealed that there are often considerable discrepancies between the proportional representation of social groups (e.g. women, the elderly, ethnic minorities) and the frequencies with which certain events (e.g. crime) are portrayed on television drama and their respective occurrences in real life. This feature of television is perhaps best illustrated by portrayals of violence and victimisation. For instance, while women, ethnic minorities and older people have tended to be underrepresented in peak-time television drama programmes relative to their respective proportions in the real world, they tend to be overrepresented as the victims of violence on television. In contrast, certain occupational groups, particularly in the fields of law enforcement and legal institutions, tend to be overrepresented. According to the analysis of Gerbner and his colleagues then, the world of television drama generally is a violent place with the chances of citizens becoming involved in crime and the likelihood of police officers having to resort to extreme violence in the apprehension of criminals being far greater than in real life (Gerbner et al, 1977, 1978).

In examining the totality of television drama, a picture emerged of a fictional world consisting of an integrated and highly complex system of characters, institutions, events and relationships. According to the Cultural Indicators model, studies of television impact which measure responses following exposure to individual programme episodes are of limited value. The effects of television cannot properly be measured with regard to any single programme seen in isolation. Instead, television changes the outlook people have on the world around them gradually over long periods of routine watching.

Television's stereotyped portrayals of groups, institutions and events presents to viewers a dramatic world with a clearly elaborated power structure in which the strong and the just are dominant, while the weak and the corrupt are suppressed or eliminated. Establishing the potential "message" content of television is only the first stage of analysis, however. The next stage must be to demonstrate the extent to which these "messages" are perceived and absorbed by viewers into their beliefs about the real world.

Gerbner and his colleagues hypothesised that habitual viewing of television drama programming with its recurring themes of victimisation among various types of characters will eventually impart information to large and otherwise heterogenous viewing publics cultivating a common system of assumptions and impressions about the social environment. There is no inclusion of other sources of influence on social perceptions within this conceptual framework.

Television is regarded as being a persuasive and highly informative medium not only in its news, current affairs and documentary output, but also in its drama which although fictional, may often provide credible, realistic depictions of people, places, events and relationships from which viewers may form impressions about the real world. But how far can it reasonably be argued that television is the only source of information people draw upon to form beliefs and opinions about aspects of the world in which they live? This important question will become the focus of discussion in subsequent chapters which report empirical findings on the relationships between television viewing and perceptions of crime.

Establishing the link

To investigate the consequences of viewing television drama's complex, integrated and frequently stereotyped system of cultural messages, a second stage of assessment was developed called cultivation analysis (Gerbner and Gross, 1976; Gross and Morgan, 1985). "Cultivation analysis tries to assess television's contribution to viewers' beliefs, behaviours, and values based on the delineation of the central and critical facts of life in the world of television. If everything people knew were learned from television drama, their perceptions of the world would differ sharply from the real world. Beliefs about population parameters, the chances for success and happiness, the likelihood of encountering violence – all are portrayed differently by TV and census statistics." (Gross and Morgan, 1985, p.226).

The assumption of cultivation analysis is that the more television people watch the more likely it is that their impressions of social reality will be coloured by television portrayals. To measure this effect, Gerbner and colleagues devised a technique in which the opinions of heavy viewers (e.g., people who reported watching television on average for more than four hours a day) were compared to those of light viewers (e.g., those who said they usually watched for less than two hours a day). Statements were given to respondents dealing with the statistical probability of occurrence of various events or with opinions about aspects of social reality to which "television answers" or "real world answers" could be given. The former were based on information about television derived from message system analysis, and the latter were taken from available statistical data sources about society.

An influence of television was inferred from the differences between the percentages of heavy and of light viewers giving "television answers" in preference to "real world answers". If this measure, called the *cultivation differential*, was significant, especially in the presence of statistical controls for the effects of demographic factors (e.g., age, sex, social class, level of education), it was taken as evidence for a cultivation effect of television.

In the context of perceptions of crime, the secondary analyses carried out by Gerbner and his colleagues during the late 1970s on data bases derived from large, national opinion surveys conducted in the United States yielded findings which they interpreted as supportive of a television influence. Exaggerated estimates of the prevalence of selected types of criminal and violent activity, when compared with real-life statistics, were much more commonplace among respondents who reported being relatively heavy viewers than among those who said they were relatively light watchers of television.

These perceptions were also linked to an emotional component, reflecting apprehension about crime. Heavy television viewing was believed to cultivate not simply distorted perceptions about personal risk but also heightened fear of involvement in crime. Since numerous content analyses had revealed the world of US prime-time television to be a violent place permeated by criminal elements, it was assumed that the dangers depicted by television would be perceived by American viewers and generalised to the real world. Once again, supportive evidence was produced. Heavy viewers exhibited greater fears of crime than did light viewers.

Several steps are required to prove empirically that this set of relationships exists. First, do individuals perceive television to be violent? Second, do viewers generalise television percepts to the real world? Third, do individuals who perceive the real world as violent also have greater fear of crime? Gerbner and his colleagues provide no evidence on these questions, but nevertheless assume that they have sufficient information from their content analysis of prime time television to be able to define one kind of response concerning fear of crime as the 'televison answer'. If, however, perceptions and feelings about the same entities do not necessarily co-vary, it is difficult to see how one can be inferred meaningfully from the other unless an empirical demonstration is provided that such a relationship actually exists. Thus, fear of crime is a highly subjective reaction and may not be easily predicted on the basis of purely objective measures of the rate of occurrence of criminal activity on television. In the chapters which follow, each of these stages will be elaborated in order to find out if such a process of influence takes place in this fashion or indeed at all.

Chapter 2

Crime on television

Measuring crime and violence on TV

Concern about the depiction of crime and violence on television is as old as the medium itself. Anxieties over the amount of violence shown on television stem from concerns that television violence can contribute to the development and display of delinquent and antisocial behaviours among viewers.

An equally controversial subject has been how to define, measure and analyse television violence. Broadcasters are frequently attacked by politicians, lobby groups and the press for not implementing tight enough controls over the showing of violence in television programmes. But controls cannot be implemented until a decision has been taken as to what it is exactly that should be controlled. How to define and measure television violence is a problem that has perplexed social scientists for many years. A number of different methods have been used. One technique is content analysis in which trained coders use specific rules and definitions to identify violence and quantify its occurrence in programmes. Traditionally, these procedures for the measurement of violence on television do not normally take into account what viewers themselves perceive to be violent. Typically, the violence of a programme is assessed in terms of the number of incidents it contains which match what the researchers themselves decide is violent. All incidents that match *a priori* definitions of violence are given equal weighting for intensity and seriousness, regardless of the dramatic context in which they occur. One must question whether viewers always agree with the researchers, however.And if they do not, it could be that such "objective" counts of violent incidents have limited value.

Another method is to obtain ratings and opinions from viewers concerning which programmes are violent and how seriously so. This can be done by asking individuals to indicate from a list of programme titles, which are violent and which are not (Howitt and Cumberbatch, 1974; Himmelweit, Swift and Biberian, 1978). One problem with this kind of measure is that it cannot indicate how much violence there is in particular episodes. Are respondents basing their opinions on one particular episode, several episodes, or the whole series?

Subjective ratings of television violence can also be made for actual programme materials. Viewers can be invited to make personal judgements about the violence contained in programme excerpts or in entire episodes. This technique allows the researcher to investigate the degree of variation in viewers' opinions about television violence and the specific ingredients of violent portrayals which affect those judgements (Gunter, 1985; van der Voort, 1986). More will be said about viewers' perceptions of crime portrayals on television in a later chapter. Meanwhile, in this chapter we will focus on objective research into the amount of crime on television.

Early research

Most people would probably agree that there is some violence on television. Determining how much violence there is presents another problem. Most researchers choose to use a descriptive content analysis technique in which clearly-defined occurrences of violence can be objectively quantified and catalogued. It is the researchers therefore who provide the definitional framework which serves as a measuring instrument which special coders are trained to use in a reliable way. The coders are taught to identify particular phenomena on screen and to record each of their occurrences in an objective fashion without placing any personal value judgements on what is seen.

The study of violence through content analysis may include an examination of many different aspects of its occurrence. For example, coders may not simply count violent incidents, but also provide a classification of them in terms of the types of programmes in which they occur, the types of characters involved, whether any weapons or special instruments of aggression were used, and the type of observable or damage or harm (i.e. to property or people) caused by the violence.

Content analyses have been used to assess levels of violence on television since the early 1950s. The first quantitative assessments of television violence were carried out in the United States. From the first, crime and violence were found to be prominent features of television prime time output.

In one study of a week's prime-time television on some New York City channels, a total of more than 3400 acts and threats were coded, averaging 6.2 violent incidents per hour. Twenty-eight percent of violent incidents occurred in crime-drama, with slightly fewer (23 percent) in westerns (Smythe, 1954). The occurrence of violence in programmes made for children was found to be even more frequent, although incidents occurred largely in comedy and cartoon contexts. In a subsequent investigation of the impact of television on children, Schramm, Lyle and Parker (1961) reported once again that violence was a common ingredient of weekday children's and prime-time programmes on TV channels serving the San Francisco area. As before though, much of the violence was found to be in comedy programmes. In their final profile of television violence, Schramm et al distinguished between incidents occurring in comic and serious contexts and included only the latter. While violent portrayals were quite numerous, exclusion of all those occurring in comic contexts resulted in a substantial reduction in the quantity of measured television violence compared with earlier content analyses in which no contextual distinctions were made.

Most early studies of the portrayal of crime and violence on television examined broadcast output at only one time. And because the methods used in different investigations often varied, meaningful comparisons between them or trend analyses over time were made very difficult. As we have noted already, however, there is a belief that the most significant influences of television are long-term ones which are contingent upon regular viewing over long periods of time. It is of interest therefore to have some indication about how the nature and amount of certain types of portrayals have changed over a number of years.

One attempt to assess violence in television over a longer period was made by Clark and Blankenberg (1972). Their analysis ran from 1953 to 1969. However, they used *TV Guide* programme synopses rather than samples of actual television output as their source material. This research therefore permitted only very generalised assessments of violence, which may have given only a very broad reflection of actual levels of violence on screen. From brief programme synopses alone, Clark and Blankenberg found a cyclical pattern to television violence, which exhibited several peaks and troughs during the period under analysis.

The most extensive and detailed content analysis of television programming that includes the study of depictions of crime and violence is the Cultural Indicators Project conducted by Gerbner and his colleagues at the Annenberg School of Communication, University of Pennsylvania. This research began in 1967-68 with a study for the National Commission on the Causes and Prevention of Violence. It continued under the sponsorship of the Surgeon General's Scientific Advisory Committee on Television and Social Behaviour, and subsequently from the National Institute of Mental Health, American Medical

13

Association, the National Science Foundation and other agencies.

The content analysis component of this project involves the monitoring of samples of prime-time and weekend daytime television for all major US networks each year. Analysis is limited to dramatic content, which means that news, documentaries, variety and quiz shows, and sports programmes are excluded during coding. A simple, normative definition of violence is employed: "the overt expression of physical force against self or other, compelling action against one's will on pain of being hurt or killed, or actually hurting or killing" (Gerbner, 1972). This definition is used by trained monitors to record the frequency and nature of violent acts, the perpetrators and victims of violence, and the temporal and spatial settings in which the acts occur. From certain combinations of these measures is derived the 'Violence Profile', which purports to represent an objective and meaningful indicator of the amount of violence portrayed in television drama.

The Violence Profile itself consists of two sets of indicators: the Violence Index and the Risk Ratios. The amount of violence occurring on television is represented directly by the Violence Index.

Essentially, this index represents the percent of programmes containing any violence at all, the frequency and rate of violent episodes per programme and per hour, and the number of leading characters involved in violence either as perpetrators or as victims. The Risk Ratios signify a character's chances of involvement in violence in television drama and, once involved, the likelihood of positive or negative consequences for him/her. The Risk Ratios too are a composite of more than one measure: the violence-victim ratio, for example, denotes chances for being an aggressor or a victim, whilst the killer-killed ratio marks the risk of killing or being killed. Both ratios are calculated within each dramatic and demographic category for a wide spectrum of character-types.

The overall picture of the world of television drama revealed by message system analysis is that it is a violent one. Gerbner, Gross Signorielli, Morgan and Jackson-Beeck (1979) reported that since monitoring first began in 1967-68, an average of 80 percent of programmes contained violence and 60 percent of major characters were involved in violence. The average rate of violent episodes was seven and a half per hour and in weekend, daytime children's programmes, violent episodes averaged almost 18 per hour. Indeed, programmes directed at children typically scored high on most measures of violence except for killing; cartoons, in particular, consistently exceeded all other categories of programmes including adult action-adventure and crime-detective shows.

The portrayal of violence by some individuals and of the propensity of others to fall victim to it was conceived by Gerbner to be a symbolic demonstration of power relationships between television characters, which could be learned by viewers and generalised by the latter to perceptions of social reality. Thus, through identifying with victims of violence, viewers might develop beliefs about the chances of their own involvement in crime in actuality.

According to Gerbner and his colleagues, measuring the extent to which various demographic sub-groups may fall victim to violence on television relates to the cultivation of concepts about chances of real personal involvement in violence. As they write in the Violence Profile No 9: "We may watch all kinds of characters to assess the general risk of involvement, but when we apply that generalised risk personally, we may be especially receptive to seeing how characters *like ourselves* (male or female, young or old, black or white, etc) fare in the world of television. Regardless of how often they do get involved in violence, if they are usually hurt or killed, the lesson learned may well be one of high risk" (Gerbner and others, 1978, p. 186).

Occurrence of crime on television

Researchers have used content analysis to investigate the occurrence on television of different aspects of criminal behaviour. Dominick (1973) examined crime and law enforcement on prime-time television programming and compared crime statistics for the world of television drama with those for the real world. He found that two out of three of the programmes he surveyed contained at least one crime portrayal. The analysis also revealed that violent crimes, such as murder and assault, are overrepresented on prime-time US television. Police are portrayed as being far more effective than they are in real life, inasmuch as television crimes are almost always unsuccessful, and criminals are nearly always caught and punished, or killed. On US television, according to Dominick's analysis, nine out of ten crimes are solved, while FBI statistics indicated that only about 23 percent of real-life crimes are solved. Television crime shows also portray police as more violent than in real life. Compared to reality, for example, criminal behaviour on television is more likely to result in a violent resolution than resolution through legal pressures. In some, despite the prevalence of crime themes in television drama, there is no close correspondence between the way crime control is portrayed as television and the way it is implemented in real life.

Packer (1968) identified two value systems or models that compete for priority in the operation of the criminal justice system. The "crime control model" sees repression of criminal conduct as the most important function of the criminal justice process. This view is that criminal conduct must be kept under tight control so as to prevent a breakdown of the public order. Public order and a high regard for criminal control is seen as an important precondition for social freedom. The Crime Control Model stresses a high rate of apprehension and correction of criminals, with a minimum of emphasis placed on ceremonious rituals and technicalities.

An alternative model is a "Due Process Model" that emphasises the rules by which suspects are treated. The Due Process Model is based upon a presumption of violence which is conceived as a directive to officials about how they should proceed. It tends to emphasise the formal structure of the law to a greater extent than the Crime Control Model. The Due Process Model emphasises the elimination of mistakes that might adversely affect individuals, while the Crime Control Model accepts the probability of some mistakes in the interest of controlling crime.

Arons and Katsh (1977) conducted an analysis of the portrayal of criminal behaviour on television. They concluded that crime shows tend to portray criminals as especially heinous and unregenerate types who deserve whatever treatment they receive from basically strong armed law enforcers. What is emphasised is support for the law under all circumstances and the idea that the machinery of justice sometimes gets in the way of law enforcement. An analysis of the content of crime shows from the perspective of constitutional law by Arons and Katsh showed that in fifteen crime shows there were 43 scenes where questions could be raised about the legality of police action. Included were 21 clear constitutional violations and 15 instances of police brutality. Summing over all this evidence it appears that television presents crime from a crime control point of view. Implicit and explicit in the content of crime shows is the message that the law should be obeyed in all circumstances.

Crime on soaps

Katzman (1972) found that crime has always been a major theme of soap operas. A more recent study by Sutherland and Siniawsky (1982) suggested that crime was becoming a more prominent form of soap opera plots. They found, for example, that murder as a moral issue was second in frequency only to deceit, and occurred more often than matters involving premarital and extramarital sex. Cassata. Skill and Boadu (1979) observed that a quarter of all deaths on soaps are due to homicides. There is a difference to the pattern of crime and criminal activity in soaps compared to action drama. Soap opera crimes may for instance take months or even years to resolve while criminals in cop series may commit their crimes and be apprehended or killed in a single episode.

Estep and MacDonald (1985) conducted a study of soap opera content which focused on the occurrence of murder and robbery, comparing the depiction of suspects and victims in daytime serials with that image derived from official records. Estep and MacDonald analysed issues of Soap Opera Digest from 1977-1984. This enabled them to identify an average of nine murders per year. Soap Opera Digests were however quite limited in the information they could provide. There was rarely any information about age, race or sex of suspects and victims and robberies and other criminal activities than murder were rarely discussed. So the authors also used informants known to be heavy soap opera viewers. Informants were asked to recall the most memorable murders and robberies they had seen on a soap opera. This information produced detailed accounts of 80 murders spread over an 8-year period. This compared with 69 murders found in Soap Opera Digests from 1977-1984. The informants recalled 78 thefts, while the Digest recounted details of only 14 robberies or other thefts.

Comparisons of the occurrence of criminal behaviour on soaps were made with their occurrence in real life. More females were depicted killing friends and lovers on soaps than occurred in real life. There was a virtual absence of blacks as murder suspects whilst one third of suburbanites in real life who are arrested for murder tend to be black. Soap opera murderers tended to be from a higher socio-economic class than real life murder suspects. As with murder suspects, fewer murder victims on soap operas were male, black and from lower social classes than indicated by official records. The mean age of murder victims (mid-30s) on soaps however corresponds to that of official records. Females were murdered twice as often on soaps as in real life.

In all, 105 suspects and 107 victims were involved in 78 incidents of robbery or theft. As with murder suspects, robbery suspects in real life are almost always male while on soap operas, a third of the suspects were female while over 90 percent of soap opera robbers were white, the FBI statistics indicated that those committing thefts in suburban areas were almost as likely to be black as white. Also real-life, suburban thieves were significantly younger than soap opera robbery suspects. There were in addition more middle-class thieves on soaps. One similar feature between fiction and real life in soaps was with regard to the kinds of objects that were stolen most often, which consisted principally of money and jewellery.

Fewer murder suspects in daytime serials had been arrested than is true of real life (62 percent against 72 percent), but more suspects were arrested for theft on soaps (36 percent) than in real life (19 percent). The appearance of realism with respect to murder on soaps, however, may be due to the serial nature of murder portrayed on these programmes. If soap opera murderers are followed to the end of their careers, which may be as long as two or three years, most are apprehended or killed by the police in the end.

Concluding remarks

Research since the 1950s has indicated that peak-time television programming frequently depicts crime or contains crime-related themes in its fictional storylines. Crime-drama series in which action centres on the behaviour of criminal elements in society and the efforts of law enforcement agencies to prevent or solve crimes and bring guilty perpetrators of unlawful acts to justice are among the most popular programmes on television. Hence, mass audiences are regularly exposed to the crime content which pervades the television schedules. Crime themes are also to be found in essentially non-crime genres of peak-time television drama output. Long-running television serials or soap operas feature crime as a prominent ingredient. Moreover, whereas crimes in crime-drama programmes are committed, investigated and usually solved within one week's episode, crimes on the soaps may take many weeks, or months, or even longer to resolve. So although there may be fewer crimes in number in soap operas than in police or detective series, those occurring in the former type of programme may be far more significant in the memories of viewers because of the length of time over which they are played out. But just how much influence does crime on television have on viewers' perceptions of and beliefs about crime in reality? Content analysis research can only provide a descriptive account of the incidence of objectively-defined portrayals in programmes. To find out about the impact of television content, we must go to the public to find out their opinions about crime and how these thoughts are related to the television programmes they report watching. It is to this issue we turn in the next chapter.

Chapter 3

Television and perceptions of crime: the American experience

Television and distorted perceptions

When developing ideas and beliefs about the world in which they live, people consider information from a variety of sources. Some of these sources consist of direct personal experience with social situations and first-hand contact with other people. In addition, information may be learned from others who relay their experiences to provide second-hand knowledge about the world. Today, however, a great deal of the available information about events in social environments near and far is transmitted through the mass media. An important question that has occupied the time and energies of many social scientists is to what extent the media have unique powers to cultivate and blend social perceptions.

In the context of discussions about public perceptions of crime, the role of the media has been given a place of prominence by some social scientists. There has been an assumption that television, in particular, with its apparently regular portrayal of crime and violence, can have a major impact on public beliefs and concerns about crime (Gerbner and Gross, 1976). But what is the scientific evidence in support of this assumption? And should any or all of the research be taken at face value or only some or none of it?

We can begin by considering some of the initial demonstrations of relationships between television viewing and perceptions of crime. In the 1970s, a series of published studies based on secondary analyses of national public opinion survey data in the United States, revealed that the amount of television respondents reported watching was correlated with certain beliefs they held about the world in which they lived. Many of the beliefs examined in this research were related to the prevalence of crime in society (Gerbner and Gross, 1976; Gerbner et al, 1977, 1978, 1979, 1980).

As we saw earlier, annual monitoring of US prime-time television revealed that its fictional drama programming was filled with portrayals of crime and violence, and populated by characters, who operated on both sides of law, who often used violent means to get what they want. In their "cultivation hypothesis", Gerbner and Gross (1976) asserted that regular exposure to this overly violent and criminal infested dramatic world conditioned in viewers an exaggerated impression of the extent of threat and danger in society and could produce excessive anxiety about personal safety.

Thus, Gerbner et al (1978) reported that while 30 percent of all characters and over 64 percent of *major* characters monitored in prime-time programming over a ten-year span were involved in violence as perpetrators, victims or both, United States census figures during this period indicated that in actuality only one-third of one percent of individuals tend to get involved in violence. The Gerbner group argue that viewers learn these content patterns, draw inferences from them and then generalise this information to their perceptions of the real world. Through their research technique called cultivation analysis, Gerbner and his colleagues found that people who watched a great deal of television, especially of dramatic, violence-oriented, action-adventure programmes, tended to endorse different beliefs about the world in which they lived than did individuals who experienced a relatively light diet of television (Gerbner and Gross, 1976; Gerbner et al, 1978, 1979). Thus, heavy television viewers tended to exhibit a measureable "television bias" in their perceptions of the occurrence of crime and violence in society and in their estimates of the number of people working in law enforcement. Heavy viewers exhibited higher estimates of likelihood of personal involvement in violence, and greater fear of being victims of crime. To set the scene it may be worthwhile to consider some actual examples.

During the second half of the 1970s, Gerbner and his colleagues reported a series of studies among American samples in which they presented evidence for links between claimed amounts of television viewing and perceptions of the prevalence of crime and violence in society, degrees of personal fear of involvement in crime, and mistrust of other people and authorities. Gerbner et al (1977) compared the answers of heavy and light viewers to questions about the occurrence of criminal violence and law enforcement agencies in society, for which two response alternatives were derived either from the quantitative programme measures generated by content analysis in the case of "television answers" or from official sources in the case of "real world answers".

The four questions posed in this study asked about personal chances of being involved in some kind of violence (TV answer – "about one in ten"; real-world answer – "about one in 100"), about the proportion of all men who have jobs, who work in law enforcement and crime detection (TV answer – "five percent"; real world answer – "one percent"), about the percent of all crimes that are violent crimes like murders, rape, robbery and aggravated assault (TV answer – "25 percdent"; real-world answer – "15 percent"), and about whether most fatal violence occurs between strangers (TV answer) or between relatives or acquaintances (real-world answer).

These four questions were presented to two samples of adults and two samples of adolescents and in every case responses indicated a significant tendency for heavy viewers to over-estimate the incidence of violence in society by endorsing "television answers" compared to light viewers. This association between amount of television viewing and perception of violence remained even after the major demographic variables of sex, age education and, in the case of one sample of adolescents, IQ, had been individually controlled. Subsequent analyses of beliefs about the magnitude of criminal and violent activities in society in relation to patterns of television viewing for two samples of adolescents in the New York area confirmed previous findings (Gerbner et al, 1979). As well as over-estimating statistical probabilities of the number of people involved in criminally-motivated violence, Gerbner et al also found a tendency for heavy viewers to give television-biased estimations on questions concerning the activities of the police. Among one sample of school-children, for example, more heavy viewers than light viewers believed that the police often use force and violence at the scene of a crime and that police officers who shoot at running persons generally hit them. Among another young sample, Gerbner and his colleagues found that heavy viewers tended to give higher estimates than light viewers of how many times a day a policeman pulls out his gun, though level of agreement with this item was much lower than for others, among all viewers. These results suggested that young viewers may be less affected by television content in their perceptions of the police than they are with respect to their perceptions of crime.

The cultivation effects hypothesis proposed that it is not only perceptions of the occurrence of crime and violence in the social environment which can be distorted by regular exposure to television's fictional world, but also the extent to which people fear being victims of crime themselves. Conceptions of social reality are believed to generalise across into the realm of affect to produce corresponding emotional reactions to perceived environmental dangers. To demonstrate this affective response, in addition to obtaining responses to questions relating to the occurrence of crime and violence, criminals and law enforcement officers in society, Gerbner and his colleagues examined data from large samples of adults and adolescents on their hopes and fears with respect to the way things are or are likely to be.

Following on from the assumption that misconceptions about the occurrence of violence in society might also give rise to a heightened sense of *fear* of violent crime in the world and the personal dangers it holds, Gerbner reasoned that if one type of response is associated with amount of television viewing, then, so too might the other more affectively-toned type of response. In order to investigate this question further, Gerbner et al (1978) computed statistical relationships between television viewing claims and fear of walking alone in the city or their own neighbourhood at night among a sample of New Jersey schoolchildren and individuals sampled in the 1976 American National Election study and the 1977 National Opinion Research Centre's (NORC) General Social Survey. Comparisons were made between the responses of those individuals who claimed to watch television for four hours or more each day and those who claimed to view for fewer than two hours. Although a greater proportion of schoolchildren than adults expressed this fear, there was a tendency throughout all samples for more heavy than light viewers to be afraid of walking alone outside at night. Thus, people who claimed to watch a lot of television were not simply more likely to overestimate the amount of danger that exists in the world than were those who claimed to be less frequent viewers, but tended also to show greater fear of their environment.

The tendency of heavy viewers of television drama to perceive a lot of violence in the real world was assumed to be reflected in turn in exaggerated feelings of mistrust and suspicion, as well as anxiety. The response dimension of mistrust was measured by existing indicators that were constructed and tested by other researchers. Drawing further upon various regional and national surveys of public opinion in the United States, Gerbner and colleagues reported that heavier viewers of television exhibited a stronger sense of mistrust and suspicion than lighter viewers (Gerbner and Gross, 1976; Gerbner et al, 1977, 1978, 1979). In the NORC's 1975 General Social Survey, for example, respondents were asked the question: "Can most people be trusted?" Comparing the answers of heavy and light television viewers, Gerbner and Gross (1976) reported that a significantly larger proportion of the former (65 percetn) than of the latter (48 percent) chose to reply that you "can't be too careful" in your dealings with others. This reply they had designated as the "television answer".

Gerbner et al (1977) expanded on the previous year's study and analysed responses to three mistrust items which had appeared in the 1976 NORC General Social Survey. The authors also added the same items to a survey of their own with children. The findings showed that heavy viewers, among both adults and children, were consistently more likely than light viewers to choose an answer which reflected a surge of mistrust and suspicion. For example, among adults, in response to the question "Do you think most people *would try to take advantage of you* if they got a chance or would they try to be fair?" Twenty-six percent of light viewers as against 38 percent of heavy viewers gave the paranoid response. When the same respondents were asked if most people can be trusted or that *you can't be too careful when dealing with people*, the latter suspicious response was given more commonly by heavy viewers (65 percent) than by light viewers (48 percent). All these results were reinforced by secondary analysis of national social survey data during subsequent years and from primary analysis of the researchers' own more localised surveys with children and adolescents (Gerbner et al, 1978, 1979).

In a secondary analysis of national social survey data, three items from Rosenberg's (1957) "faith in people" scale were related to data on the television viewing behaviours of the same national sample (Gerbner et al, 1978). Gerbner called this syndrome "mean world" and found that heavy and light viewers differed substantially in their beliefs that people "would try to take advantage of you if they got a chance", that "most people cannot be trusted" and that people "mostly are just looking out for themselves". Answers to these questions were found to be significantly related to reported amount of television viewing even when other facts such as age, sex education and income were controlled. However, there were differences between ethnic minorities. Blacks did not show this relationship between viewing behaviour and "mean world" perceptions to the same extent as did whites, with the exception of those who were well-educated and in higher income groups, for whom the usual cultivation effects did exist. This result suggested that there may be certain subcultural differences in sensitivity or susceptibility to television's cultural messages. Middle-class blacks with better education and higher incomes may be attitudinally similar to whites in many respects and also may live in similar social and physical surroundings. The latter conditions may be more important to the way they perceive the world around them than is their television watching. Lower-class (poor) blacks, on the other hand, tend to live more often in run-down neighbourhoods where crime and violence abound, and their fears and feelings of mistrust and hopelessness may stem from more powerful roots than television portrayals. Although Gerbner and his colleagues were careful to control for several possibly confounding factors such as sex, age and educational level of television viewers, other researchers whose work will be examined later have suggested these may not be the only or the most crucial "third variables" whose influence should not be ignored in this context (Doob and Macdonald, 1979; Wober and Gunter, 1982).

Two challenges to Gerbner's findings

In their initial publications, empirical support for their cultivation effects thesis was obtained by the Gerbner group through secondary analysis of national public opinion survey data bases. In 1980 two important papers were published, one by Hughes and the other by Hirsch, in which they re-analysed these same data bases in an effort to replicate Gerbner's original findings and conclusions. Using extensive methodological and statistical controls for extraneous variables on which information concerning survey respondents was available but not taken into account by Gerbner, both Hughes and Hirsch failed to replicate much of Gerbner's evidence for television cultivation effects.

Hughes (1980) criticised the Gerbner group's work of the late 1970s on two important counts: first, for having omitted controls for available variables which might reasonably be expected to produce relationships between television viewing and social perceptions and, secondly, for failing to control for extraneous variables simultaneously instead of one at a time. Hughes re-analysed the same data as those used by Gerbner et al (1978) from the 1975 and 1977 General Social Surveys and included controls for relevant variables ignored by the Gerbner group. Amongst the control variables were age, sex, race, income, education, hours worked (per week), church attendance and size of home town. Some of these variables were significantly related to amount of television watching even in the presence of statistical controls for the others, while some were not. For example, an initially strong relationship between sex of viewer and television viewing disappeared when controls were employed for hours worked per week. This indicated that women watch more television than men perhaps because they are likely to work fewer hours outside the home than men. Further such analyses led Hughes to conclude that the exclusion by Gerbner et al of race, hours worked and church attendance from their 1978 analysis may have been quite a serious one.

On relating five social perceptions examined by Gerbner and his colleagues with amount of television watching whilst controlling simultaneously for a range of demographic factors, Hughes (1980) found that only one of the five relationships claimed by Gerbner et al (1978) still held up. Fear of walking alone at night was found to reverse the direction of its relationship with amount of viewing, indicating that those individuals who claimed to watch television heavily were *less* likely to be afraid of walking alone at night in the neighbourhood.

Hughes discovered a number of items included in the NORC's General Social Survey not reported by Gerbner et al, which provided response patterns counter to the cultivation hypothesis. With one such item ("Are there any situations you can imagine in which you would approve of a man punching an adult male stranger?") Hughes found that, when controlling for sex, age and education, there was not one instance, overall or within each demographic division, when "heavy" viewers were more favourable towards physical violence than "medium" or "light" viewers. Within many demographic groups, the proportion of "heavy" viewers who expressed a distaste for violence was significantly higher than among lighter viewers. In Hughes' own words such findings raise "the possibility that in failing to ensure cross-sample comparability, introduce multiple controls, and report items where the data do not support the argument for television's "cultivation" of beliefs and attitudes, the Annenberg group has itself contributed to distorting scientific reality" (1980, p.18).

Hirsch (1980) questioned the work of the Annenberg group mainly on three counts. First, he argued that Gerbner's categorisation of viewing behaviour is arbitrary and selective. Secondly, there are unreported attitude responses on the original data bases which do not support the model Gerbner presents. Thirdly, there are ambiguities in Gerbner's reported data and in the way these data are presented.

Analysing the Annenberg group's violence profiles 9 and 10 (Gerbner et al, 1978, 1979), Hirsch pointed out that although these reports read as though there is consistency across samples in the way viewers were categorized (i.e. as "heavy" or "light" viewers), a close examination of the research procedures revealed that as many as six different weight of viewing classifications had been used across different samples and used interchangeably. In violence profile 10, for example, children from their New Jersey school sample were coded as 'light' viewers if they reported viewing an average of three hours of television daily. Children from a comparable New York school sample who reported this much viewing were coded as "heavy" viewers. Hirsch believed there were serious problems with making the same assumptions about "heavy" and "light" viewers from different samples when the way they have been defined varies from one sample to the next in this way.

In a thorough re-analysis and re-classification of the original NORC sample used by Gerbner and his colleagues, Hirsch included two new categories: non viewers (zero hours viewing) and extreme viewers (8+ hours). In their writings up to this time the Gerbner group had made the major assertion that heavier viewers, in response to the lessons they had supposedly learnt from television, were likely to have higher scores on items tapping fear of victimisation, anomie and alienation, Hirsch, however, found that on many of these items *non-viewers* had higher scores than light, medium, heavy or extreme viewers. The few people who watched no television at all turned out to be more fearful or alienated than any television viewers. According to Hirsch, this result clearly runs counter to the cultivation hypothesis, which posits that the responses of those who are exposed to television's messages the least which should be closest to the real world.

Hirsch next turned his attention to the other end of the viewing scale, and compared the responses of "heavy" (4-7 hours viewing daily) and "extreme" viewers (8+ hours daily) on a series of NORC items which had previously been analysed by Gerbner. Hirsch found that the demographic composition of these heavy viewing divisions were different. Markedly higher proportions of "extreme" viewers than "heavy" viewers were women, housewives, retired workers or black, lower class and less well educated. The "cultivation" hypothesis proposes that people who watch the largest amounts of television will provide television-biased answers to survey items more often than people who watch for fewer hours each day. Hirsch divided Gerbner's "heavy viewers" into two sub-groups of heavy and extreme viewers, in order to test this hypothesis and also the reasoning behind collapsing both of these types into a single category. The results indicated that extreme viewers provided "television answers" *less often* than heavy viewers on 11 (61%) of the 18 NORC/Gerbner items that Hirsch re-analysed. Extreme viewers provided "TV answers" most often on three anomie items ('the lot of the average man,' bringing children into the world', and 'public officials being indifferent'), on one Gerbner "mean world" item ('people try to be fair'), and also on a suicide item and an alienation item.

Hirsch issued a further challenge to the Gerbner group on the grounds of ambiguity and contradiction with regard to their position on cultivation analysis as causation. On the one hand, while they seemed to reject the efficiency of the old-fashioned 'hypodermic model' of cause-effect analysis when attempting to explain the nature of television's influences on viewers, at the same time they failed adequately to distinguish obvious conceptual similarities which exist between causal analysis and cultivation analysis as they have defined it. Cultivation analysis had consistently followed the procedure of introducing single controls for age, sex and education on the relationship between television viewing and selected social perceptions. But, such is the inherent complexity of relationships of this sort that multiple controls for these variables are essential for reliable tests of hypotheses. Therefore, Hirsch employed multiple controls on the NORC data to examine the Gerbner contention that television viewing exerts a "separate and independent contribution to conceptions of social reality within most age, sex, educational and other groupings".

Following an earlier example set by Gerbner et al (1978), Hirsch combined particular groups of items and questions to form indices of mistrust of others, alienation, fear of crime and attitude towards physical violence. In five of the six indices, there was consistent evidence to show that heavy viewers were more likely than light viewers to provide "television answers". Light viewers yielded "mean" or "scary" world responses the least and both non-viewers and medium viewers were generally more likely to give such answers. But, after adjustment for the other variables, the percentages of heavy and extreme viewers giving the "television answer" followed no pattern at all. In one case where an apparent cultivation effect did appear, it moved in the opposite direction to that proposed by the cultivation hypothesis. Heavier viewers exhibited smaller supposed cultivation effects. In only one out of the six indices ("mean world") was the difference in responding between heavier and lighter viewers in the direction predicted by the cultivation hypothesis.

Neither Hirsch's criticisms nor his method of re-analysis of the data base used by the Gerbner group have been universally accepted. According to some researchers in this field, there are sufficient problems with Hirsch's analyses to question the validity of his claimed disconfirmation of the cultivation hypothesis. Hawkins and Pingree (1982) raised the point that non-viewers and extreme viewers may be highly unusual individuals who can probably be distinguished in terms of numerous specific attitudes other than their out of the ordinary television viewing patterns. Consequently, the fact that the beliefs of these peculiar individuals did not exhibit the customary television cultivation influence identified by Gerbner and his colleagues does not preclude the possibility of such an influence occurring among the remaining 90 percent or more of the population falling within the light, medium and heavy viewing categories.

Hawkins and Pingree (1982) also suggested that Hirsch's procedure for controlling third variables may still leave open the possibility for a relationship between television viewing and social reality that is independent of such interrelated demographic variables. Even if a positive correlation between reported amount of viewing and a social perception is reduced to zero because of education's relation to one or the other, sub-groups identified by their levels of education can still differ in the associations they exhibit between viewing and perceptions of social reality. Indeed Gerbner et al. (1980a), in response to both Hirsch and Hughes, reported that different kinds of relationships between television viewing and social beliefs exist within different demographic sub-groups that run counter to one another. They thus cancel each other out when the demographic variable in question is statistically partialled out and consequently severely weakens television cultivation effects in the population as a whole.

Mainstreaming and resonance

Gerbner and his colleagues have argued that within the cultivation analysis framework, it is the overall *amount* of television viewing which is the important indicator of the strength of television's influence on people's ways of thinking and acting. For heavy viewers, television is the dominant source of information about the world – overriding all other sources. An underlying assumption here is that heavy viewers will be more likely than light viewers to give "television answers" to questions concerning their opinions about social objects or events. However, substantially different patterns of association between viewing and social beliefs can often emerge for different social groups. Hughes (1980), for example, found that when controlling for demographic or environmental factors which previously had not been taken into consideration, such as local crime levels, number of hours worked per week, and size of town of residence, relationships between viewing behaviour and social beliefs became considerably weakened. Furthermore, Hughes showed that when controls for these and other demographics such as age, sex, socio-economic class, race and education were implemented simultaneously, no overall cultivation effects emerged. In reply, Gerbner, Gross, Morgan and Signorielli (1980a), however, argued that no *overall relationship* does not mean the same as *no relationship at all*.

More detailed analyses of data from a more recent survey gave rise to the introduction of two new labels to apply to the differences in cultivation effects between social groups: (1) *mainstreaming* which indicates a diminution in cultural differences among heavy viewers and (2) *resonance* which refers to special cases in which television's depictions of reality are congruent with a typical segment of the general population's actual or perceived reality, which purportedly leads to a marked enhancement in cultivation effects (Gerbner, Gross, Morgan and Signorielli, 1980b). Let us look a little more closely at how these two patterns of influence operate. It is known, for instance, that more educated or higher income groups have the most diversified patterns of social and cultural opportunities and activities. And, on the whole, they also tend to be relatively light viewers. Consequently, they are less likely to endorse television-biased answers to opinion items. But there are some heavy viewers *within* the higher education/high income groups and these people respond differently. Their social perceptions tend to be more like those of other heavy viewers, most of whom have less education and income. According to the mainstreaming hypothesis, it is the college-educated, high-income *light* viewers who diverge from the mainstream, i.e. the relative "commonality of outlook" that television tends to cultivate; heavy viewers across all social strata tend to share a relatively homogeneous outlook.

Television's influence on public beliefs about social reality, however, does not only consist of the cultivation of a common outlook on the world; it also functions to enhance the salience of specific issues, objects or events. This effect is called resonance. In Gerbner et al's own words, "When what people see on television is most congruent with everyday reality (or even *perceived* reality), the combination may result in a coherent and powerful "double dose" of the television message and significantly boost cultivation" (1980b, p.15). In other words, where patterns of events depicted on television are consonant or in harmony with patterns of similar events in reality, the two message systems "resonate" so as to amplify their salience to an observer. In response to criticism of their earlier analyses and interpretations by Hughes (1980), Gerbner et al (1980b) reanalysed some of their data to illustrate the two phenomena of mainstreaming and resonance.

Mainstreaming. The phenomenon of mainstreaming was examined in relation to the cultivation of fear of victimization, interpersonal mistrust and anomie. Using a question concerning one's chances of being involved in violence in any given week, once again heavy viewers were found to be significantly more likely to give the television-biased answers. But there were also important differences between certain social groups. A large majority (80 percent) of both light and heavy viewers with low incomes gave the higher risk response, and showed no evidence of a relationship between viewing behaviour and response to this item. Examination of middle and upper-income groups, however, revealed that the proportion of light viewers giving the "television answer" was much lower. Light viewers with middle and upper-bracket incomes were considerably less likely to express a high expectation of encountering violence, while heavy viewers with middle or high-incomes exhibited almost the same level of perceived risk as the low-income group (Gerbner et al, 1980b).

In another analysis, three items were combined by these writers to form a "mean world" index which measured the degree to which respondents agreed that people are just looking out for themselves, that you can't be too careful in dealing with people, and that most people would take advantage of you if they got the chance. Overall, television viewing was found to be significantly associated with the tendency to express mistrust. What is more interesting, however, is the relationship between television viewing and interpersonal mistrust for specific groups of the population. The relationship was strongest for respondents who had had some college education, even though these individuals were in general less likely to express interpersonal mistrust than non-college-educated people. The most striking contrasts emerged from the comparison between whites and non-whites. As a group, non-whites tended to have stronger "mean world" beliefs than did whites. Yet when the relationship of these beliefs to viewing behaviour was considered there was a significant *negative* association among non-whites between television viewing and mistrust. In contrast, there was a significant positive association among whites. Thus, say Gerbner et al, "... those groups who in general are *least* likely to hold a television-related attitude are *most* likely to be influenced toward the "mainstream" television view; and those who are most likely to hold a view *more* extreme than the TV view may be "coaxed back" to the "mainstream" position" (1980, p.18).

Similar patterns emerged for relationships between amount of viewing and feeling anomia. Combining into a single index three of Srole's (1956) anomia items (the lot of the average man is getting worse; it is hardly fair to bring a child into the world; and most public officials are not interested in the lot of the average man) it was found that the best indicator of anomia was education. That is, less well-educated respondents expressed stronger feelings of anomia than the better educated. When the association between television viewing and endorsing statements of anomia was examined within educational subgroups, this relationship still persisted for those (college-educated) respondents who, as a group, were far less likely to express anomia in their general attitude to life. For those individuals with less education, who were relatively alienated to begin with, television viewing had no apparent relationship with anomie. Again, these results implied that television cultivates a convergence of outlooks towards its "mainstream".

Resonance. The second important refinement of the original cultivation theory was that television-biased beliefs will be most pronounced when aspects of the social environment are congruent and thereby "resonant" with television drama profiles. As noted earlier, not all attempts to reproduce the cultivation findings of the Gerbner group have met with success. In a study with residents in Toronto, Canada, Doob and MacDonald (1979) attempted to replicate earlier American findings indicating that television causes people to overestimate the amount of danger that exists in their own neighbourhoods, whilst controlling for a previously uncontrolled factor – the actual incidence of crime in the respondent's neighbourhood.

Respondents in a door-to-door survey indicated their media usage and estimated the likelihood of their being a victim of violence. Neighbour-hoods were chosen so as to include a high and low crime areas in central Toronto and two similar areas in the suburbs of the city. When actual incidence of crime was controlled, no overall relationship emerged between television viewing and fear of being a victim of crime. Across the four areas of the city, those individuals who watched the most television or violent programming tended to be those who were most afraid, but within each area this relationship did not always hold. Whilst it was present within the high crime area of the city, it tended to disappear in the other areas.

Doob and MacDonald interpreted their data as evidence of the spuriousness of the relationship between television viewing and fear of crime in the real world. However, Gerbner and his colleagues (1980b) have suggested instead that for those urban dwellers who live in high crime centres, television's violent imagery may be most congruent with their real life perceptions. People who thus receive a "double dose" of messages that the world is violent, consequently show the strongest associations between viewing and fear.

Gerbner et al analysed the responses of a large national sample to five questions which were combined together to form a Perceptions of Danger index. They also made a distinction similar to that of Doob and MacDonald between residents living in low and high crime neighbour-hoods. It was assumed that respondents who lived in the larger cities and who had low incomes were likely to reside in areas with relatively high crime rates, while high income urban and high and low income suburban residents arguably lived in less dangerous areas.

It was found that a significant relationship between amount of television viewed and perceptions of danger emerged in the presence of controls for demographic factors for low income and high income residents of suburban areas, and also for low income urban dwellers. No such relationship occurred for high income urban dwellers. The strongest cultivation effects emerged for the low income city residents and this was interpreted as evidence for "resonance" whereby people who already lived in areas where crime levels were presumably high had their fears of falling victim to such crime enhanced by watching a great deal of (violent) television drama.

A further example of this resonance effect was evidenced in beliefs about the victimization of the elderly. Content analysis of television drama programming had previously shown that old people tend to be victims of crime more often than young people in TV fiction. But while a significant relationship between amount of television viewing and tendency to think that old people are most likely to be attacked was found among older respondents, no such association occurred among young or middle-aged respondents. Resonance is said to occur when a feature of the world of television drama has particular relevance or salience for a part of the television audience.

In recent studies, certain of Gerbner's colleagues have carried out their most comprehensive and complex analyses yet of associations between television content profiles and public perceptions of the social environment. Morgan (1984) reported an analysis of relationships between risk-ratios for different demographic sub-groups as portrayed on television and correlations between perceptions of victimization among those same sub-groups in the real world and the amount of their television viewing. Morgan divided up his television character and survey populations according to five demographic categories: age, sex, race, social class and marital status. These were five demographic characteristics for which risk ratios had been computed and which also provided easily measurable real world parallels. Interactively, these mainly dichotomised categories generated 323 analytically distinct sub-groups.

In the analysis, the dependent variable was the *relationship* expressed as a correlation coefficient, between amount of viewing and perceived chances of victimization within each of these sub-groups. The independent variables were the percentages of television characters in a given sub-group who commit violence or suffer violence, and the risk ratio (percent of perpetrators divided by percent of victims of violence) within each sub-group. Morgan examined the degree of association between the independent and dependent variables for each demographic sub-group.

Results showed in general that in terms of perpetrators and victims, as the percentage of characters in a group who are shown on television as perpetrators goes up, the partial correlation between amount of viewing and perceived chances of involvement in violence goes down. Viewers whose television counterparts are more aggressive show smaller associations between how much they watch and their perceptions of real-world risk. At the same time, the more that viewers see characters like themselves as *victims*, the *greater* the cultivation of a heightened sense of danger. In terms of non-fatal violence, the real-world groups who show the strongest evidence of the cultivation of a sense of risk are both less violent and more victimised on television. There was virtually no association between the degree of audience cultivation and the percent of killers, but a completely different relationship appeared for the percent who are killed, particularly among major characters. The more viewers see leading characters like themselves killed (not just hurt), the weaker the association between amount of viewing and their perception of danger.

Morgan says this may be an artifact of the relatively unusual and special status of major characters who are killed on television. Few leading characters are killed in most groups – indeed in many none at all are killed. When those groups in which substantial numbers are killed are examined alone, however, positive correlations emerge between television killings and the cultivation effect. Morgan states that: "From multidimensional clusters of demographic matchings, we see that television is most likely to cultivate exaggerated perceptions of the likelihood of victimization among those viewers who *see their fictional counterparts as least powerful*" (p.376). But a crucial question here is where is the evidence from this or any other cultivation-effects study that viewers do actually "see" their fictional counterparts or any other aspect of television in one way or another. At no stage does the Cultural Indicators Model, as employed by the Annenberg group, ever test in a direct fashion how viewers perceive television content and interpret the social meanings it supposedly conveys.

Another problem with the model which persists even through such a complex analysis as Morgan's is the assumption that viewing is largely non-selective and therefore that the relationship between social attitudes and beliefs, and television usage is uni-directional. Not all viewers fill their viewing time with the same programmes. One viewer, whether heavy or light, may not watch the same kinds of programmes as another viewer. Thus the content seen, information absorbed, and messages learnt from television may vary considerably across viewers.

Another hypothesis is that television viewing is not an antecedent of fear of environmental dangers at all, but is a consequence of it. People who are more afraid may stay indoors and watch more television (Zillman and Wakshlag, 1984), possibly sometimes to learn how to cope with crime (Mendelsohn, 1983) or simply to ease their fears (e.g. Boyanowsky, 1977). This selective-viewing hypothesis is pertinent not only in the context of fear-of-crime but also in connection with other areas of social perception. In a later chapter this hypothesis will be examined in greater detail and evidence will be presented which indicates that, although television may reinforce certain beliefs about the world, viewing behaviour may itself be influenced by existing constellations of attitudes and beliefs viewers bring with them to the viewing situation.

Concluding remarks

During the 1970s, a group of American researchers led by Gerbner investigated relationships between the amount of television people claimed to watch and the beliefs they held about the incidence of crime and violence, together with their fears of personal victimisation. On computing secondary analyses on national opinion survey data over several years, Gerbner and his co-workers claimed to have demonstrated reliable relationships between patterns of television viewing and perceptions of crime, whereby heavier viewers perceived more crime and violence in the real world than did lighter viewers, and exhibited greater fear of crime than did the latter. These results were taken as evidence for a *cultivation effect* of television. In other words, individuals who watched greater amounts of television and who therefore also saw greater quantities of crime-related content, developed beliefs about levels of crime and personal danger in society which reflected the portrayed risks and dangers on television. These results and the conclusions drawn from them were not readily accepted by all researchers, and two in particular threw down serious challenges to the Gerbner analyses. Questions were raised about the adequacy of controls for extraneous characteristics of viewers which might offer other explanations for the apparent relationship between amount of television viewing and beliefs about crime, and in the presence of statistical controls for which the latter relationship disappears or is severely weakened. Questions were raised also about the way in which viewers were classified as relatively heavy or relatively light viewers. The definitions or dividing lines were not always the same across different surveys. And yet 'heavy' and 'light' categories at a conceptual level were treated as equivalent even across surveys in which they were operationally defined in different ways. In ironing out these problems, re-analysis of the data originally used by Gerbner, did not always produce the same results.

Gerbner responded to these criticisms by introducing two concepts – mainstreaming and resonance – through which he argued that the continuous effects of television were more subtle than at first envisaged. They could occur to differing degrees or even in different directions across different demographic sections of the audience. Therefore, simple statistical controls for these extraneous factors might serve artificially to reduce relationships between television viewing and perceptions of crimes or fail to reveal the nature and strength of such relationships within different parts of the audience. Conceptually at least this counter-theorising answered some criticisms of the original cultivation analyses, though not all. An alternative explanation of the relationships between social perceptions and television viewing is that the former are antecedents of the latter, rather than the other way around. A third compromise account is that the relationship works in both directions and that social perceptions and selective viewing of certain types of television content can be mutually reinforcing. An assumption which is made by the latter hypotheses, however, which marks another significant departure from the simple cultivation effects account, is that overall television viewing is a less important factor than are the specific types of programmes that are watched. Television viewing may indeed be related to perceptions of crime, but only with respect to levels of watching specific areas of crime-related content.

Chapter 4

Television and perceptions of crime: evidence from other countries

Before we turn to examine research evidence for the extent and nature of television's influence on beliefs about crime and violence in Britain, some attention will be given briefly to cultivation effects studies conducted in other countries outside the United States, where in all cases both American and British programmes occupy not insubstantial proportions of the television schedules. These countries include Canada, Australia, the Netherlands and Sweden.

We begin with US neighbour, Canada. Canadian research on whether television viewing affects public perceptions of crime is particularly interesting because viewers in Canada can receive all three major American television networks in addition to their own indigenous broadcast and cable television channels. While there may be degrees of similarity between available television diets in Canada and the United States, to what extent do television audiences in the two countries exhibit similar patterns of relationships between their viewing patterns and their beliefs about levels of crime and violence in their respective social environments.

In a survey carried out among adults living in Toronto, Doob and MacDonald (1979) tested beliefs about the incidence of crime and violence in society. On a 37-item questionnaire respondents were asked about the personal fear of falling victim to crime, their perceptions of the likelihood of victimisation among other social groups, the need to take precautionary measures against crime and estimates of the incidence of crime in Toronto. All of these perceptions were related to self-reported information about their television viewing patterns. The researchers built in another important variable, however, and this was the location where respondents lived. The sample was recruited from residents in four locations around the city which were classified in terms of crime levels and centrality. These were residents from high-crime inner city areas, low-crime inner city areas, high-crime suburban areas and low-crime suburban areas.

Doob and MacDonald found that relationships between television viewing and social perceptions differed in the extent to which the latter specified detailed events or possibilities. For example, more specific fear-of-crime positions such as being afraid to walk alone at night for fear of being the victim of a violent crime, believing that the chances were high that a close friend would be the victim of burglary in the next year, or believing that an unaccompanied woman is likely to be attacked in a subway station late at night were only either weakly related or unrelated to total amount of television viewing or amount of television violence viewing when the effects of local crime rates were statistically controlled. But responses to more general (i.e. less personal) questions such as "Do you think that it is useful for people to keep firearms in their homes to protect themselves?", "Should women carry a weapon such as knife to protect themselves against sexual assault?" and estimation of the proportion of assaults or murders committed by or directed against minority groups, tended to be more powerfully related to reported television viewing behaviour, even in the presence of controls for levels of neighbourhood crime. It is possible then that matters of a less personalised nature are affected by television portrayals more than are items having to do with a person's own level of fear. This is a factor we will return to in more detail in the next chapter.

Through a series of complex procedures of statistical analysis, Doob and MacDonald found that perceptions of crime and violence could be condensed to four categories of beliefs. The first of these was a fear-of-crime dimension which expressed levels of concern about crime in society and especially about personal chances of falling victim to it. This set of anxieties about crime was found to be related to reported amount of television viewing and amount of viewing violence-laden programmes. Across all four sampled areas of the city, it was found that people who watched the most television or television violence tended also to be those who were most afraid. This relationship was not the same within all areas, however. Although it held up in high crime areas, it tended to much weaker in other areas.

Further examination of the data revealed interesting linkages between television viewing and beliefs about crime among certain kinds of people. Those people who did not see much local neighbourhood crime, who did not believe that it is unsafe for children to play alone in a park, and who were not afraid of personal attack, but were afraid of being burgled, tended to be females living in low-crime city areas. People who were afraid to walk alone at night but who did not feel they would be victims of a violent crime, however, tended to be females living in high-crime city areas. One explanation could be that their fears reflected their local environment and resulted perhaps in their taking extra precautionary measures to protect themselves from attack such as avoiding certain areas at certain times. The fact that they had taken such measures could, in turn, contribute to the belief that these actions reduced the likelihood of personal victimisation.

Finally, people who believed that unaccompanied female subway riders and children playing alone in parks were vulnerable to attacks, but who felt safe themselves and believed their neighbourhoods to be safe were suburban dwellers who watched a lot of TV violence. Personal safety here probably reflects the relative security of their comfortable suburban environment as learned through direct personal experience, but fears about attacks on lone female subway riders (perhaps something of which they had less direct experience) may reflect images shown on television.

In summary, although there were some initial indications that television viewing was related to perceptions and fears of crime, these relationships largely disappeared or were substantially modified when other more basic factors (in particular area of residence) were taken into account. The actual incidence of crime in the neighbourhood emerged as an important factor which is closely linked with individuals' beliefs and anxieties about crime. The fact that television viewing was related to perceptions of crime more so in high-crime rather than in low-crime areas might, suggest Doob and MacDonald, indicate that television violence has differing levels of relevance for people living in different parts of the city. Televised portrayals of crime may have less significance for people living outside high-crime areas, because for these individuals the amount of television watched bears little or no relationship with the perceived likelihood of being a victim of crime. Although controlling for neighbourhood of residence modified the relationship between television watching and fear of crime, it did not consistently eliminate the relationship between television viewing and other perceptions of crime which dealt with more factual matters (e.g. incidence of crime, likelihood of involvement for others). Hence, although television may provide individuals with a source of information about crime, it does not necessarily affect their views of how afraid they should be.

The Australian experience

In drawing comparisons between television's cultivation effects in the United States and in Australia, Pingree and Hawkins (1980) replicated and extended the Gerbner approach to show relationships between television viewing levels and perceptions of the occurrence of violence in society and feelings of inter-personal mistrust ("mean world"), among over 1200 Perth schoolchildren. Four Violence-in-Society items were the same as those analysed by Gerbner et al (1977), tapping beliefs about chances of involvement in some kind of violence, the percentage of Australian men who have jobs as police officers or detectives, whether most murders are committed by strangers or relatives or acquaintances of the victim, and the percentage of all crimes involving violence, such as murder, rape, robbery and assault. The "mean world" index consisted of three items: if they got the chance, most people would try to cheat me; you can never be too careful in dealing with people; and mostly, people are just looking out for themselves. Opinions given by the children on the latter items indicated that heavy viewers had a much more cynical outlook on the world than did light viewers. The relationship between total amount of viewing and the number of television-biased responses about the incidence of violence in Australia was very strong. Even when single and multiple controls for demographics and the perceived reality of television were employed, relationships between television viewing and violence in society and mean world remained.

Pingree and Hawkins also examined relationships between viewing certain types of programme and children's views about the real world. They found that perceptions of how much violence there is in society were strongly related to viewing crime-adventure shows, cartoons and game shows, while lack of trust in other people was relatively weakly related to viewing these programmes. Viewing crime-adventure shows, however, was related to both sets of beliefs. One further interesting finding to emerge was the fact that children's perceptions of the way society appears in Australia (as against corresponding perceptions of the United States) were related more closely to how much they watched imported American programmes than to their viewing of other foreign imports or programmes produced by local television networks.

The finding that viewing of certain types of programmes may influence particular beliefs about society reinforces the argument that messages conveyed by television may produce impressions about the real world that are consistent with the nature of television content, especially among people who are particularly heavy viewers. If such cultivation effects result from learning fairly specific lessons from television, then those programmes whose content is informationally most relevant are probably the ones most likely to produce the strongest television influences.

Pingree and Hawkins' results suggest that the effects of television programming on beliefs about the social environment may extend beyond the culture or country in which that content is produced. But this conclusion may be rather too generalised. It is possible that there are sufficient similarities between Australian society and American society in certain important respects for the same television content to have replicable effects across these two countries. The question of whether American--produced TV programming, especially popular crime-adventure series, will exert similar effects on the ideas people in other countries have about society has not so far been unequivocally answered. As we have already seen, research in Canada, a society which has much in common with the United States, has indicated that television's effects on beliefs about and fears of crime may be dependent upon, or weak in comparison with, other important factors which characterise citizens and where they live. As we will also see in a later chapter, research among British populations has indicated that television has at most only weak effects on such beliefs in this country and that these are related more especially to viewing of particular programme types than to overall amount of television seen. Furthermore, statistical controls for differences in certain personality characteristics of viewers often reduces the relationships between television viewing patterns and perceptions of crime to practically nothing.

The Dutch experience

Research into the cultivation effects of television modelled closely on the American work by Gerbner and his colleagues was carried out during the late 1970s in two European countries other than Britain. The results of this work from the Netherlands and Sweden were published in the proceedings of an international symposium on Cultural Indicators in a volume edited by Melischek, Rosengren and Stappers (1984).

In the Netherlands, the research consisted of a content analysis of television output to establish the prevalence of violence on Dutch television programming and of a survey to investigate relationships between television viewing and beliefs about crime and violence in society. Bouwman and Stappers (1984) reported the Dutch Violence Profile investigation which analysed four weeks of programming across ten broadcasting organisations in the Netherlands during prime-time (8.30 – 10.00 pm) and before prime-time when family and children's programmes were shown.

They found less violence in Dutch television on the whole than had been reported earlier for American television. Using the Gerbner system of content analysis, programmes broadcast during family viewing time were in particular less violent than American counterparts. However, the Violence Index for Dutch crime programmes during prime-time was comparable with that for prime-time programmes in the USA. Crime programmes on Dutch television at this time were mainly imported from Britain and Germany, with just a handful originating from the United States.

Looking further at the relative degrees of risk of being a victim of violence on Dutch television among particular social groups, Bouwman and Stappers found that females were more vulnerable than males in line with findings from the United States. Unmarried men were more likely to commit violence, while married men were more likely to be killed. The elderly were the most vulnerable group on Dutch television, while young adults were most likely to be killers. In the United States, Gerbner and his colleagues have argued that patterns of portrayals such as these carry certain social messages or meanings which can be learned by viewers and absorbed into their beliefs about the world around them. To find out if there were any relationships between social beliefs and television viewing, Bouwman (1984) conducted a telephone interview survey with some 600 people in the Netherlands. Self-reported amount of television viewing was related to responses on a number of items which dealt with "images of violence and attitudes of mistrust" (p 407).

The television viewing measure was derived from two questions "How many days a week do you watch television" and "on those days that you watch, how many minutes do you watch?" The social beliefs items dealt with levels of trust in or mistrust of other people, perceptions of women's and elderly persons' likelihood of victimisation, perceptions of whether crime is increasing, knowledge about whether most killings occur between strangers or people who know each other, and the need to learn to defend oneself. These were largely derived from earlier studies by Gerbner and others (e.g. Doob and MacDonald, 1979; Gerbner et al, 1979; Pingree and Hawkins, 1980).

Upon applying simultaneous statistical controls for the education, age, sex and type of residential location of respondents, Bouwman reported that six out of 19 social perceptions or opinions were still significantly related to reported amount of television viewing. In his table of results, however, only five significant correlations are actually shown. Four of these items concerned perceptions of reality, such as whether most killing takes place between strangers or friends, and only one dealt with feelings (e.g."you can never be too careful in dealing with people"). According to Bouwman, the cultivation of fear of crime by television does not seem to be strongly evident among Dutch people.

Bouwman also conducted analyses among different demographic sub-groups to compare across them for relative strengths of relationships between claimed amount of television viewing and perceptions and fear of crime. In this analysis he wanted to find out if there was any evidence for the phenomena of mainstreaming or resonance about which Gerbner had talked in the United States. Bouwman found some evidence of a possible resonance effect when comparing younger and older adults (above and below the age of 37) on one item only, which related to killings between strangers. There was a greater divergence of opinion as a result of weight of viewing among older than among younger viewers. According to Gerbner, resonance occurs when a feature of television has special salience or relevance for a particular group of viewers. There was no evidence either of mainstreaming or resonance among any of the other results however.

The relative absence of cultivation effects among Dutch viewers is discussed by Bouwman in connection with a number of factors. He suggests first of all that the influence of television programmes, especially of drama, is limited in the Netherlands because the Dutch do not depend on television as their main or dominant information source with regard to their beliefs about the real world to the extent that people in the United States may do. Secondly, the media in the Netherlands have different roles, with regional and local newspapers for instance carrying international and national as well as local stories, while in the United States this does not happen to the same extent. Thirdly, the programme mix of the television schedules is more varied on Dutch television than on American television because broadcasting organisations are forced by law to offer a varied programme diet. Fourthly, the opportunity to watch television is smaller in the Netherlands because there are fewer television channels and they broadcast for shorter hours than is true of the United States. This may in turn account partly for the fact that television plays a less important role in the Netherlands than in the United States as a source of entertainment and information about the world.

Bouwman also suggests that, although the amount of violence on Dutch television in some areas of programming is almost the same as on American television, when measured in fairly narrow "objective" terms, the nature of that violence is different. Thus, violence on Dutch television may carry different meanings for its viewers than the violence on American television does for American viewers. An objective system of content analysis, however, does not measure the meanings acquired by viewers from television programmes, and so cannot properly demonstrate these differences.

The Swedish experience

Swedish television shows very little violence, so one would suppose that there is little opportunity for beliefs or fears about crime to be strongly affected by it. Nevertheless, researchers in Sweden have joined in the

41

effort to find out if there is any such influence, especially among young people. Hedinsson (1981) and Hedinsson and Windahl (1984) reported such an analysis among children and adolescents aged between 11 and 15 years. Information on television viewing habits and beliefs about crime were collected during part of a larger project called the Media Panel Research Programme. This longitudinal study was conducted during the late 1970s and early 1980s to study young people's media use and the influences of media among teenagers in Sweden. Data were collected three times in 1976, 1978 and 1980, from approximately 1,000 children and adolescents each time. In addition to measures of how much television they watched, the teenagers were asked about their degree of involvement with the programmes they watched. This was measured with items such as "when I watch a TV programme that I like, I sometimes wish I was part of the action". Answers to these television questions were then related to social perceptions, some of which dealt with beliefs about crime and violence derived from earlier studies by Gerbner and his co-workers.

Results showed that the amount of time spent watching television had only weak links with some perceptions. Amount of viewing was not as important as degree of involvement with television, which was related to perceptions of crime, but then only among older adolescents. Among the youngest respondents (aged 11). television viewing was unrelated to crime perceptions, but among the oldest (aged 15) involvement with television programmes was linearly related to their perceptions of social violence. High involvement in the television content consumed was associated with exaggerated perceptions of how much crime and violence there is in society. The strongest relationship was between a retribution index (the size of prescribed penalty for seven different kinds of crime added together) and amount of viewing. According to the researchers, this suggested that it may be people with a stronger sense of punitive justice who seek to watch more television, rather than that television violence (of which there is significantly little) induces fear and suspicion.

Hedinsson and Windahl call for more emphasis to be given to the conception of the active viewer in future research on television's cultivation effects. The findings reported in this chapter that the kinds of content rather than simply the overall amount of television to which people are exposed is often more precisely and significantly related to their perceptions of the social environment bears testament to this need. Viewers may be influenced in their perceptions of the real world only by that television content which is perceived to be informationally relevant to those aspects of social reality under consideration. In the next chapter we examine in more detail the significance of the perceptual differentiations viewers can make between different kinds of programme content and between television portrayals and real life experience as factors which mediate and limit the cultivation effects of television on perceptions of real life crime and violence.

Concluding remarks

Researchers in several countries, other than the United States, have investigated relationships between television viewing and perceptions of crime in indigenous populations. Their findings have not consistently replicated American results. In some cases results similar to those in the U.S. have emerged, while in other cases zero relationships have occurred.

This may mean that some cultivation effects are national rather than international phenomena. In the Dutch case, for example, the use and degree of reliance on television is not the same as it is in the U.S. Furthermore, the more strictly regulated broadcasting system ensures a more varied programme menu in the Netherlands than is found in the U.S. Failure to replicate original American cultivation effects even among a population which is exposed to largely the same programmes, as in Canada, however, gave rise to explanations other than the cross-national transference of cultivation effects. Once again, question-marks hang over the conceptual and methodological frameworks of the Gerbner work, which lead to doubts about the robustness of the original American results. Relationships between television viewing and perceptions of crime may be mitigated by actual levels of crime in the location where people live. This is not to say that televised crime may not work in synchrony with real-life crime to affect beliefs and concerns about crime. Although, as we will see in the next chapter, the ways in which people perceive and make judgements about crime on television and in the real world can be quite sophisticated and when these comparisons are taken into account, the strength and range of television's influence on what people believe about the world around them are shown to be quite limited.

Chapter 5

Television and levels of judgement about crime

The cultivation perspective which puts the argument that television can influence the public's beliefs about crime has not been universally accepted by mass communications researchers. An alternative view proposed by Zillmann (1980), for example, postulates that, if anything, the effects of viewing television programmes which feature crime-related themes could be the opposite to that indicated by the Gerbner group. Because there is little reason to expect people to view material which produces aversive states such as fear, and because crime programmes on television invariably feature the triumph of justice – in crime drama the bad guys are usually caught and punished in the end – individuals who watch these programmes should find comfort and reassurance through them.

Support for this position is provided by Gunter and Wober (1983) who found a positive relationship between beliefs in a just world and exposure to television crime drama programming. This finding conflicts with the contention that viewing crime drama cultivates fear and mistrust and leaves open the possibility that what is cultivated instead (or in addition at least) are perceptions of a just world. It also leaves open the possibility, however, that those who believe in a just world seek to support these beliefs by more frequent exposure to crime drama on television.

Recent research has indicated that, regardless of the direction of casuality inferred from correlational links between television viewing and perceptions of crime, demonstration of the nature and significance of television's contribution to these anxieties and beliefs requires a more sophisticated model of influence than that put forward by Gerbner and his co-workers. Increasing recognition has been given to four additional elements which represent important enhancements to the original cultivation effects model.

First, relationships between levels of exposure to television and perceptions of crime may be programme specific. In other words, any influence of television on beliefs about crime may depend not so much on the total amount of television viewed per se, but more significantly on how much informationally-relevant programmes (i.e. those with crime-related content) are watched (Weaver and Wakshlag, 1986).

Secondly, the influence of television may depend not simply on what is watched but on how viewers perceive and interpret the content of programmes (Teevan and Hartnagel, 1976; Pingree, 1983). Even programmes with crime or law enforcement themes may have little impact on beliefs about crime in real life, if viewers are not prepared to recognise such programmes as having a true reflection on everyday reality (Potter, 1986).

Thirdly, judgements about crime can have different frames of reference. Tyler has made a distinction between two kinds of judgements people make about crime (1980, 1984; Tyler and Cook, 1984). First, there are judgements at the societal level which refer to general beliefs about the frequency of crime in the community at large. Then there are personal judgements which refer to beliefs about personal vulnerability to crime and one's own estimated risk of being victimised. Tyler found that these two levels of judgement were not related to media experiences. Estimates of personal risk were primarily determined by direct, personal experience with crime (Tyler, 1980; Tyler and Cook, 1984).

Fourthly, at either one of these two levels, the perceived likelihood of other- or self-involvement in crime or the concern about such involvement are situation-specific and may not be the same from one setting to the next. Tamborini, Zillmann and Bryant (1984), for example, demonstrated that fear of crime is not a undimensional construct. As well as the personal level-societal level distinction, fear of crime in urban areas was found to differ from fear of crime in rural areas.

Television exposure patterns

Much of the early research on the role television plays in shaping public perceptions and attitudes regarding crime depended on non-specific measures of television viewing. In general, viewing measures did not differentiate between exposure to different kinds of television content. While the homogeneity of programming on prime-time schedules on the major US networks may mean that differential indicators of viewing by programme-type are not necessary, the same cannot be said with regard to viewing in other countries, such as the UK, where peak-time programming tends to be much more varied.

Consideration of levels of exposure to different areas of programming clearly becomes important when crime-related content is found to occur in some types of programmes and not in others. Obviously, crime-dramas whose major characters are police officers or private detectives may be relevant to perceptions of crime because their storylines centre on criminal activities and law enforcement. The news media also provide extensive coverage of different kinds of crime. Content analysis of newspapers and television news have indicated that crime stories are regularly reported in both (Graber, 1980; Skogan and Maxfield, 1981; Gordon and Heath, 1981).

Just as fictional drama on television tends to overrepresent the occurrence of crime (Gerbner et al, 1977, 1978, 1979; Lichter and Lichter, 1983), so too the appearance of stories about crime in the news has been observed to be disproportionate to actual incidence of crime. In particular, the news media tend to report violent crimes, such as murder and rape, far out of proportion to their actual occurrence, as compared to other types of crime such as burglary and white-collar crime (Graber, 1980; Skogan and Maxfield, 1981). To what extent then does level of exposure to one or other of these categories of programming, as distinct from exposure to other types of output, such as non-crime-related drama or current affairs, or light entertainment shows, relate to perceptions of crime in reality. And within news media or within programme types that deal with crime-related matters, the types of crimes reported or depicted may vary, together with the way they are described, explained and presented. Are public perceptions of crime differentially responsive to these different media portrayals of crime? Recent research suggests that they are. People may be sensitive to and affected by media crime portrayals of one type, but do not respond to portrayals of another type.

Skogan and Maxfield (1981) found no relation between fear of being a victim of crime and reported amount of viewing television news (or reading about crime in newspapers) among urban residents in the USA, when statistical controls were applied for the effects of respondents, age, education, race and sex.

In two studies of the impact of newspaper crime reports on fear of crime, Heath (1984) differentiated between different types of reports. Previously global analysis of newspaper crime coverage had assumed that all crime reports are equally fear-provoking, but this assumption is misleading. In her first study, Heath classified 36 newspapers according to the proportion of crime reports that involved local crimes, sensational crimes and random crimes. Levels of fear of crime were then assessed among a random sample of readers of these newspapers. Respondents who read newspapers that printed a higher proportion of local crime news reported higher levels of fear if the crimes were predominantly sensational or appeared to be random, whereas respondents whose newspapers printed a low proportion of local crime news reported lower levels of fear if the crimes were predominantly sensational or random. These findings were replicated in a second study in which college students who read reports of local crimes expressed higher levels of fear if the crimes were random rather than part of organised crime, whereas the opposite pattern occurred with regard to non-local crimes. In the local context, incomplete information about random crimes might lead the reader presumably to believe that such incidents could affect anyone. If, however, there were extraordinary circumstances, for example, a revenge gangland killing, the reader would realise that it was crime of a sort unlikely to affect him or her. In the non-local context, there is some evidence from this study that the worse the crime environment seems to be elsewhere, the safer the reader feels in his or her own environment.

In a secondary analysis of data gathered for a study of the public impact of crime prevention information campaigns, O'Keefe (1984) examined relationships between claimed exposure to television, crime-drama on television and to crime news on television and several categories of crime perceptions. The findings provided no support for the proposition that total time spent watching television is related to public perceptions and attitudes regarding crime, or that television viewing per se increases fear of crime. Furthermore, the amount of time spent watching crime entertainment programmes was similarly unrelated to nearly all the crime perceptions examined in this study. However, claimed watching of crime news on television was significantly associated with some crime perceptions. In particular, perceptions of neighbourhood danger, perceived likelihood of being a victim of crime, and the extent of worry over being victimised were all positively related to reported exposure to televised news about crime.

Bryant et al (1981) presented groups of respondents with a controlled television viewing diet for a six-week period. At the outset of the experiment respondents were divided into low and high anxiety types on the basis of responses given to items from Taylor's Manifest Anxiety Inventory. Low anxiety and high anxiety individuals were randomly assigned to one of three viewing conditions: (1) light justice-depicting, (2) heavy justice-depicting and (3) heavy injustice depicting action-adventure programming. Justice-depicting programmes concluded with a clear triumph of justice or good over evil, while in injustice-depicting programmes, order was never truly restored. The viewing diet was controlled inside the laboratory, but outside, at home, respondents were free to watch whatever and whenever they pleased.

After six weeks of controlled laboratory viewing, anxiety, fearfulness and other social belief measures were also taken. Respondents were also told that tapes of six action-adventure series were held in stock and they were invited to view these programmes further as part of a study on television formats. The number of these programmes viewed during this subsequent stage provided a measure of voluntary selective exposure to action drama.

Results showed that both amount and type of viewing affected viewers' anxiety levels. Light viewing and heavy-justice viewing produced a slight increase in anxiety levels among low-anxiety individuals – but resulted in a reduction of anxiety in individuals already highly anxious. For heavy viewers of programmes in which injustice was habitually depicted, both low and high anxiety individuals exhibited significant increases in anxiety, with the greatest increment occurring for those who were already highly anxious. Individuals high in anxiety at the outset also held stronger beliefs that they would at some time be victimised than did those initially low in anxiety. For both groups, however, a heavy diet of action-adventure material, with or without justice, resulted in increased perceptions of victimisation. As for *fear* of victimisation, as distinct from its *perceived likelihood*, Bryant et al found that viewing television injustice produced significantly greater increase in fearfulness than did television justice. Heavy viewers of action-adventure programmes who saw repeated incidents of restoration of justice also rated their chances of vindication in the event of personal victimisation greater than did injustice viewers.

Differential perceptions of TV content

Research has shown that viewers can be highly discriminating when it comes to portrayals of violence, crime and law enforcement on television. Audiences are capable of making clear distinctions between how certain social entities (such as criminals or the police) are depicted on television and how they appear or are believed to be in real life. Viewers do not always read the same meanings into television content as do researchers, and this is especially the case where portrayals of crime and violence are concerned. These television portrayals are not invariably taken at face value. Indeed, audiences can often exhibit a level of sophistication in the judgements they make about television programmes that is underestimated or not taken sufficiently into account by some research paradigms employed to demonstrate the so-called 'cultivation effects' of television on viewers' attitudes and behaviour.

One area in which this last point can be clearly illustrated is the measurement of television violence and its meaning for viewers. We are told that violence is commonplace on popular television drama programming (Gerbner and Gross, 1976; Gerbner et al, 1977, 1978, 1980; Morgan, 1984; Signorielli, 1984) but how salient is it for viewers? We are often told that there is too much violence on television, but violence for whom, the critics, the researchers or the viewer?

Although it may be impossible to define exactly what the audience in general means by 'violence', there is evidence to suggest that viewers' perceptions do not accord strongly with objective counts of programme incidents. Research has shown that structures such as those monitored in content analysis are not always perceived by ordinary viewers as salient attributes of programmes. For example, a content analysis of British television output, using a fixed definition of violence, showed that the rate of violent incidents per hour was four times as great for cartoon shows as for any other type of programme (Halloran and Croll, 1971), while a study of the audience's perceptions of television violence indicated that cartoons were not rated as particularly violent (Howitt and Cumberbatch, 1974).

Even in films with human characters, violent scenes may not feature as important aspects of content and viewers may often fail to mention violence in discussions about films containing violent action shortly after viewing, unless specifically asked about such content. In a field study conducted by audience researchers at the British Broadcasting Corporation (1972) viewers were asked to fill out a questionnaire about specific programmes shortly after they had been broadcast, in which reactions to violence and other aspects of programme content were probed. It was found that perceptions of programmes as *violent* did not depend on the actual number of violent incidents. Nor was there any strong relationship between perceiving a programme as violent and verbally reported emotional arousal. Assessment of violence as unjustified, however, was associated with negative evaluations of the programme. Most respondents also claimed that 'realism' was an essential element in their perceptions of televised violence, with violent real-life events reported on news bulletins or shown in documentaries generally rated as more violent than violence portrayed in fictional settings. Although this study can be regarded as little more than exploratory, it nevertheless indicates that viewers' personal assessments of television programmes are determined by many different content factors, of which violence is only one, and by no means the most important. Recent research has revealed that adults and children alike are capable of highly refined judgements about television violence. Viewers have their own scales for deciding the seriousness of incidents and their opinions do not always agree with researchers' categorisations of violence (Gunter, 1985; Van der Voort, 1986).

Adults' perceptions of TV violence. Instead of deciding in advance what violence is, or is not, these researchers allowed viewers themselves to decide about the seriousness of violence contained in various functional television portrayals. Gunter (1985) reported twelve experimental studies in which groups of people were shown scenes taken from British crime series *(The Professionals, The Sweeney)*, American crime series *(Kojak, Mannix, Starsky and Hutch)*, westerns *(Alias Smith and Jones, Cannon for Cordoba)*, science fiction series *(Buck Rogers, Star Trek)* and cartoons *(Mickey Mouse)*.

Viewers were invited to make a variety of personal judgements about each scene along a set of qualitative rating scales. Scenes were shown singly or in pairs for comparative judgement, in a small lecture theatre. Variations in perceptions of the scenes were examined in relation to a number of things; the types of programmes the scenes came from, the types of weapons or instruments of violence that were used, the physical setting of the action and the degree of observable harm the violence caused to victims in each scene. The results indicated that viewers may be significantly influenced in their personal opinions about television violence by many different attributes of television portrayals.

Familiarity of surroundings is one of the most powerful factors influencing viewers' perceptions of television violence (Gunter, 1985; Gunter and Furnham, 1984). The closer to home the violence is portrayed as being in terms of place and time, the more serious it is judged to be. Thus, it was found that violence in British crime series was generally rated as more violent than similar portrayals on US series of the same type. Portrayals of 'violent' behaviour in cartoons or science fiction programmes, however, were seen as essentially non-violent.

Perceptions of television violence were also found to vary significantly with a number of other characteristics of televiion portrayals. The kinds of fictional characters who inflict the violence, how the violence is inflicted, and how much harm is done to those on the receiving end, all emerged as important mediators of viewers' opinions about television violence.

Some of the results, however, were paradoxical. Opinions about violence perpetrated by law enforcers and by criminals, or by men and by women, were markedly different, depending on the types of programmes from which they came. With extracts from British crime series, for instance, viewers were most concerned about violence inflicted by men upon women, while in scenes from American series they were concerned more by women being violent to men (Gunter and Furnham, 1985). In an American context, violence performed by criminals was perceived in more serious terms than that used by law enforcers (usually the police), while in British settings it was law enforcer violence that viewers were more troubled by (Gunter, 1985).

One can only speculate at this stage as to the reasons why these differences in opinions occur. One answer may lie in the societal norms regarding the use of violence. Traditionally, society approves of some forms of violence under certain circumstances, and disapproves of others. For example, violence used by police officers to uphold the law, or that used by private citizens in self-defence against an attacker are, within certain limits, permissible. Under these circumstances, however, the use of violence must not far outweigh the magnitude of the behaviour of the law-breaker or attacker. Where the force used to repel an attacker is much greater than that justified by initial provocation, violent retaliation will not be found so acceptable.

The other interesting way in which characterisation was related to perceptions of television violence was in connection with differential opinions about violence perpetrated by males and by females. Among the kinds of violence of which society most disapproves is that performed by men, the physically dominant and stronger sex, against women, who are generally regarded as physically weaker. Since violent television portrayals set in contemporary British locations are closer to home for British viewers than those set in contemporary American locations, perceptions of violence in familiar British settings involving British characters may be strongly influenced by norms of conduct that prevail in the society in which British viewers live. Thus, a violent attack by a male character on a female character in a British programme will be judged according to the appropriate norms of conduct and rated as unacceptable. Similar types of portrayals in American crime series, however, are sufficiently distanced from the everyday reality of British viewers for the same rules of judgement not to apply. Instead, such factors as the frequency and familiarity of particular types of portrayal within these programmes, but not in relation to everyday life, may be more important mediators of opinions about them. Since most violence in American crime programmes is perpetrated by men, the rather unusual experience of seeing it used by women is relatively more disturbing. Of the different physical forms of violence, shootings were seen as most violent, but stabbings, with their close-in ruthlessness, were perceived as most frightening and disturbing particularly in British programmes (Gunter, 1985; Gunter and Furnham, 1984).

Children's perceptions of TV violence. Van der Voort (1986) conducted a study of children's perceptions of TV violence at three schools in Holland. In all, 314 children were shown full-length episodes of eight television scenes. The episodes varied from realistic crime drama *(Starsky and Hutch and Charlie's Angels)* to adventure series *(Dick Turpin and The Incredible Hulk)* and fantasy cartoons *(Scooby Doo, Tom and Jerry, Popeye and Pink Panther)*. Immediately after showing each programme a post-exposure questionnaire was filled in measuring ten perception variables: (1) readiness to see violence, (2) approval of violent actions seen in the programme, (3) enjoyment of the violence seen, (4) evaluation of the programme, (5) emotional responsiveness, (6) absorption in the programme, (7) detachment while watching, (8) identification with the programme's chief characters, (9) perceived reality of the programme and (10) comprehension and retention of programme content.

Van der Voort investigated whether programmes perceived to be realistic were also more absorbing for children who would thereby respond to them with more emotion and less detachment than they showed towards programmes perceived to be more fantastic. Thus, *Starsky and Hutch* and *Charlie's Angels* were perceived to be realistic, while *The Incredible Hulk, Dick Turpin* and cartoons were seen as fantastic. Realistic programmes were watched with more involvement, more emotion and less detachment. The two crime drama series mentioned above were regarded as containing the most violence of any of the programmes the children were shown.

Van der Voort found in fact that nine- to twelve-year olds' judgements of the amount of violence programmes contain differ little from those of adults. He makes the important point, however, that "children's violence ratings do differ from those of content analysts who analyse the amount of violence a programme contains by means of the systematic observation of programmes recorded on videotape. Programmes that are extremely violent according to "objective" content analysis can be seen by children as hardly containing any violence."(p.329). Thus, although content analyses have identified cartoons as being among the most violent of television programmes in terms of numbers of objectively identified incidents per hour or per show (Gerbner, 1972; Gerbner and Gross, 1976), such programmes tend to be seen by children as containing hardly any violence at all.

On the basis of the above findings both with adults and children, it is clear that viewers classify programme content differently from the descriptive analysis of research frameworks which employ narrow definitions of violence. There would seem to be some merit in recommending a subjective approach rather than a purely objective one in the analysis at least of televised violence, because this perspective enables one to identify the programmes which viewers themselves take most seriously. A subjective approach outlines ways in which differential weights of seriousness can be applied to programmes. This leads usually to the classification of programmes that are perceived as most true to life as also being the most serious in the violence they depict.

Comparisons of criminals and law-enforcers on TV and in real life. Similar perceptual distinctions are made by viewers with regard to the portrayal of law enforcers on television. Even fairly early on, researchers observed that law enforcement or law occupations were highly visible on television drama. De Fleur (1964) found in one analysis of American television that one-third of occupations depicted on fictional programming were connected with the law. The police on television more often than not lead glamorous lifestyles and are very good at their job. Criminals usually get caught and are brought to justice. But how much of this is actually believed by viewers?

Comparisons of what people think about television cops and the police in real life have shown that the two versions are not generally perceived in the same way. Rarick, Townsend and Boyd (1973) for example examined non-delinquent and delinquent adolescents' images of real life and television police. Respondents indicated the extent to which they felt that each of 36 statements accurately described the way television or real life police are or operate. Six distinct patterns of perceptions emerged; three of actual and three of television police. Perceptions of actual police were diverse, ranging from highly favourable to openly hostile, with some mixed feelings in between. Perceptions of television police were relatively homogeneous and positive. Among both the delinquent and non-delinquent adolescents there was widespread belief that television police were idealised dramatisations different from the real thing. Those youngsters who had favourable impressions of actual police tended to see greater similarity between actual and television counterparts than did those who held unfavourable impressions of actual police.

However, delinquents did not on the whole see greater differences between actual and television police than did non-delinquents, despite their greater contact with the police in actuality.

British research among members of the general public has also found that viewers do not naturally accept television depictions of the police. Tannenbaum (1979) conducted a project while on attachment to the BBC's Broadcasting Research Department, on audiences' reactions to a docu-drama series about the work of police detectives in Britain. *Law and Order* was a series of four plays broadcast on BBC2 in spring 1978 which attempted to depict in a realistic fashion the kinds of interactions that occur between police and criminals, as well as members of the legal and penal professions. The programmes were designed to give an idea of the way CID detectives operate.

In order to find out if the series had any impact on viewers' perceptions of detectives and the way they work, groups of individuals were recruited through the membership of the BBC Listening and Viewing Panel in London to take part in viewing sessions in which they saw an episode from the series. One of the areas of interest was the effect that programme labelling would have on how viewers responded to it. For some participants therefore the programme was described as a drama, while for others it was said to be a documentary.

There was one principal character featured in the programme, a detective inspector, who was an obvious focus of attention and provided a television portrayal against which impressions about real life detectives could be compared. It emerged that there was no confusion between the depicted detective in the programme and the audience's own image of the typical CID officer they would expect to find in reality. Respondents were able comfortably to make this distinction. Nor was there any substantial change in beliefs about real life detectives contingent upon watching the programme.

Labelling the programme either as a documentary or a drama made little difference to viewers' perceptions in this study, although Tannenbaum conceded that the conditions under which this differential labelling was implemented were less than optimal and may not have been sufficiently well done to produce the expected effect on audience perceptions. When asked subsequently to give their personal reactions, however, viewers for whom the programme had been described as a documentary tended to see it as an accurate reflection of detectives' lives more so than did those individuals to whom it was presented as a drama.

TV – reality discrimination and TV influence. As we can see, viewers can be very discriminating about the things they see on television. Portrayals of crime, violence and law enforcement are not all perceived as being alike, nor are they necessarily accepted as accurate reflections of reality. What difference do these perceptions make to relationships between what people watch on television and their real life beliefs? Are those people who are more discriminating about television less likely to be influenced by its content. The answer appears to be yes.

Teevan and Hartnagel (1976) surveyed teenagers aged 12 to 18 years to find out the possible effects of television violence on their perceptions of crime and their reactions to such perceived crime. These researchers, however, distinguished between the objectively-defined content of programmes such as counts of numbers of bodies or violent incidents shown on screen, and viewers' subjective perceptions of how much violence is contained in a programme. Thus, although a programme might objectively be said to contain certain kinds of incidents, are these incidents actually salient for and perceived by viewers? And if programmes are perceived as being violent, do viewers see the violence as an effective means of achieving goals or overcoming problems?

Having obtained information from the teenagers about how much television they usually watch and which programmes they like to watch best, Teevan and Hartnagel classified the youngsters' favourite programmes for levels of portrayed violence and statistically related the perceptions of crime in society with their reported television viewing patterns.

There was little relationship between viewing programmes independently defined as violent and either perceptions of crime or reactions to it.
Thus, if these teenagers perceived a great deal of crime and were afraid of
it, regardless of whether or not they had directly experienced it, their
perceptions and fears were not strongly associated with the particular
television entertainment programmes they liked to watch most. However,
when the youngsters themselves defined their favourite shows as violent,
then these perceptions were more strongly related to their beliefs about
the amount of crime in the real world and their fears of it.

Specifically, those teenagers who perceived their favourite television
programmes as violent also perceived more crime in their own neighbourhood, in the downtown area of the city in which they lived and in and
around school. Such viewers were also more likely to report carrying
something to defend themselves and regarded it as more likely that they
would at some time have to defend themselves. Even in these cases
though the degree of association between television viewing measures
and beliefs about social crime levels were weak.

Perceived reality of TV and TV influences. Potter (1986) examined the
effects on relationships between amount of television exposure and
estimates of real world evidence of controls for perceived reality of TV
content. He examined three types of reality perception:

— *Magic window* – degree to which a viewer believes TV content is an
   unaltered, accurate representation of actual life. TV is a "magic
   window" which presents beautiful pictures of the world. People who
   score low on this dimension think of TV content as a highly stylised
   form of communication that presents fantastic settings and characters
   which are very different from those in real life.

— *Instruction* – television as an instructional aid which augments and
   expands their direct experiences. People at one end of this scale
   believe that TV programming, even if it is fictional in nature, presents
   useful moral lessons which help them work through problems
   victoriously and learn how to cope. At the other extreme are people
   who believe that the fictional situations in TV programmes are so
   unusual and distorted that they can see no usefulness in drawing
   parallels to their own lives. So, they do not expect to learn anything of
   importance from TV.

— *Identity* – degree of identity the viewer perceived between TV
   characters and situations and the people and situations experienced
   in real life. It is the degree to which viewers feel that TV characters
   could fit into their real, everyday lives.

In the presence of demographic controls there was no evidence of a relationship between amount of TV viewing and perceptions of victimisation rates.

Individuals who scored high on magic window reality exhibited the instruction effect, while the low group exhibited a reverse effect so that higher amounts of viewing were associated with lower estimates of victimisation. When individuals were grouped according to their scores in the Instruction and Identity dimensions, the instruction effect was generally among those in the low groups.

Comprehension of TV and TV influences. As well as the perceived realism of programmes on television which carry crime-related content, the impact of television on young viewers' beliefs about social reality may also be mediated by their ability to follow the storyline of a television drama. Learning from television may depend among other things on the way individuals watch and are able to comprehend the content before them on the screen. Research has shown that the ability to remember facts from television programmes and to draw inferences which go beyond the explicit content in programmes both improve with age through early and middle childhood. Findings indicate that children younger than eight have great difficulty keeping track of the order and relationships between events in a plot separated in time, but are able to follow them when they occur close to each other (Collins, 1973, 1979).

Furthermore, Collins has pointed out that drawing implications is a crucial skill for adult-like understanding of typical television plots. Thus, much of what is crucial to plot comprehension never appears or is not stated explicitly and there is evidence that children do less well with implicit than explicit content, although performance does improve with age (Collins, 1982).

In more recent work with children aged between 10 and 12 years Pingree (1983) has found that ability to follow a television storyline may have important implications for the influence of drama programmes on young viewers' beliefs about the real world. Children in this study answered questions about viewing habits and social reality beliefs, which included questions about the perceived prevalence of violence and criminal behaviour. Two weeks after this initial questioning they watched an edited television programme and were asked questions about it. The children were then divided on the basis of their scores on the latter exercise into those who were good and those who were poor at following the story and at being able to understand how one part of the story was related to another part.

Although across the sample as a whole, greater reported amounts of television viewing by the children were associated with exaggerated perceptions of crime and violence in society, there were important differences between children who were good and bad at following a programme storyline. What emerged was that children who were good at following the programme exhibited weaker associations between their reported viewing and their social beliefs than did children who were poor at programme comprehension. Indeed, it was only among the latter that substantial correlations between viewing behaviour and social perceptions occurred. Furthermore, it also emerged that children who were good at programme comprehension held a more integrated and coherent outlook on the world than did other youngsters. Pingree suggests that young viewers who are better able to follow television storylines are probably more active viewers. It seems likely that such children think more about what they are watching on television and perhaps make more comparisons with other available sources of information about such things as crime and violence. Alternatively, such children may be more discriminating and knowledgeable about television itself, and even though they may have no direct experience of crime, choose not to believe fictional representations anyway.

Levels of judgements about crime

Recent research has indicated that not all judgements about crime are equally susceptible to media influences. A distinction can be made between different types of perceptions of crime and safety and between different fear states.

At a conceptual level, a distinction has been made between personal- and societal-level judgements. Most of the early studies of television viewing and perceptions of crime focused mainly on societal-level judgements – those that deal with population estimates and the general state of the environment for the individual. This type of study attempted to demonstrate the effect of media exposure on beliefs about the prevalence of violence in society and on mistrust of other people and authority (Gerbner et al, 1977, 1978; Neville, 1980). Other studies examined relationships between reported television viewing and personal-level perceptions concerning judgements of personal likelihood of involvement in crime and personal fears of victimisation (Doob and MacDonald, 1979; Gerbner et al, 1978, 1979). At no time, however, did any of these investigators make the conceptual distinction between personal- and societal-level judgements or attempt to distinguish differential effects of television exposure in relation to each type of judgement.

In a subsequent experiment, Tamborini, Zillmann and Bryant (1984) extended the work of Bryant et al (1981) and attempted to overcome certain methodological shortcomings of the earlier study. Whilst Bryant et al measured the effects of a particular viewing diet immediately after the final programme, Tamborini and his colleagues employed delayed, as well as immediate, testing to examine long-term effects of exposure to television crime content. Tamborini et al also distinguished effects at a number of different judgemental levels, e.g. whether increased concern about violence related specifically to the individual at a personal level or more generally for society at large. These researchers also examined the possibility that enhanced fearfulness was not a generalised reaction but was specific to certain situations.

Experimental participants viewed one of four videotaped programmes: a non-violent episode of *The Love Boat* (control); a version of the TV movie *High Midnight* in which the bad guys were punished (justice-depicting); a version of the movie in which the bad guys go unpunished (injustice-depicting); or a thirty-minute crime-documentary on crime in Harlem, New York. Respondents' perceptions were assessed either immediately after viewing or three days later, along a series of items designed to distinguish several dimensions of apprehension.

A factor analysis on perceptual items revealed that fear of crime is a multidimensional construct. Fear in urban areas is distinguished from fear in rural settings. Fear for personal safety is distinct in people's minds from fear for someone else. Furthermore, estimates of risk from crime represent a different sort of judgement from fear of victimisation. Therefore, to consider fear of crime as a singular disposition which individuals exhibit equally across all situations fails to represent its true character. We may be fearful of crime in one situation but not in another. We may fear for others but not for ourselves.

Results showed that watching different types of crime and violence had different effects on social perceptions at different levels, and that these effects usually dissipate over time. Only viewing of the crime documentary appeared to have a more lasting impact on perceptions. Tamborini et al were also able to demonstrate that fear of crime or victimisation may be situation specific. The researchers were able to distinguish fear in urban areas from fear in rural settings, and fear for personal safety from fear for someone else.

This research indicated that viewing a certain kind of television programme dealing with crime can influence certain social perceptions while leaving other associated judgements unaffected. For example, watching the crime-documentary and the injustice-depicting crime drama led to more exaggerated "perceptions of crime" and fear of assault in urban environments. Watching the injustice-depicting crime-drama also increased manifest anxiety, while viewing the crime documentary also elevated fear for one's spouse or close partner. However, no effects were found of watching these programmes, or any of the others, on personal fear or fear of assault in rural environments.

These results were consistent with earlier survey research indicating that media effects on perceptions differ at personal and societal levels (Skogan and Maxfield, 1981; Tyler, 1980). They were also consonant with theories of social cognition which suggest that different aspects of our knowledge about the world may be segregated into separate storage compartments. And any changes that might occur to one set of beliefs or feelings about the world consequent upon new information received (e.g. from the media) may not spread to effect changes to other sets of beliefs or feelings stored elsewhere (Reyes, Thompson and Bower, 1979; Srull and Wyer, 1979; Wyer and Srull, 1980). Thus, watching certain kinds of television programmes may induce changes in the extent of perceived danger in the social environment for others but may not extend to influence beliefs about dangers for oneself. Furthermore, changes in social perceptions may only be responsive to media content that is directly relevant in the kind of information it conveys to the perceptions in question. Thus, television programmes depicting crime in urban settings affects viewers' perceptions of crime in urban locations but has no impact on their perceptions of crime in rural locations.

Personal experience with crime

Although the authoritative view of the linkage between television viewing and social perceptions depicts information conveyed by the medium as so pervasive that other potentially influential environmental sources appear secondary (Gerbner and Gross, 1976; Gross and Morgan, 1985; Morgan, 1983), there is substantial reason to consider television as only one of several unique information sources which are differentially utilised and weighted by individuals when forming perceptions about the causality of events and the state of their environment (De Fleur and De Fleur, 1967; Reeves, Chaffee and Tims, 1982; Singer, 1980; Wyer, 1980).

There is, for example, a broad volume of evidence indicating that the social perceiver distinguishes between at least three sources or modalities of information relevant to perceptions of personal vulnerability:
(a) direct, personal experiences;
(b) experiences of others (i.e. relatives and friends) interpersonally conveyed as factual information;
(c) experiences of others presented through the mass media as either factual information (e.g. news reports) or in an exaggerated, distorted or entirely fictional form (e.g. crime drama).

Also it appears that social perceptions are formed and reinforced on the basis of the highest order experience available (i.e. direct, interpersonal or mediated). When direct experience is lacking or highly ambiguous, however, the individual is most susceptible to the suggestion of indirectly obtained information, conveyed either interpersonally or through the mass media (cf. Hawkins and Pingree, 1982; Zillmann, 1979).

Fazio and his colleagues (e.g. Fazio and Zanna, 1981) demonstrated in a series of experiments that social perceptions based on direct, experimentally obtained information, were held with greater confidence, strength and clarity than were similar perceptions based upon indirect experience. As a result, these perceptions strongly influenced all subsequent stages of topic relevant information processing (i.e. attention, interpretation, elaboration and memory retrieval).

This pattern of effects also has been observed in several studies. These studies have found that direct experience as the victim of a personal crime (i.e. assault, robbery, rape, theft) elevates significantly estimates of and concerns for future personal victimisation (Friedman, Bischoff, Davis and Person, 1982; Garofalo and Lamb, 1978; Skogan and Maxfield, 1981) and mediates the perceived credibility or reality of subsequently received information (Elliott and Slater, 1980; O'Keefe, 1984; Tyler, 1980; Tyler and Rasinski, 1984).

Similarly, interpersonally conveyed experience in the absence of direct experience, has been shown to heighten individuals' perceptions of both their own and others' vulnerability to negative events (e.g. getting cancer or being mugged), whereas individuals without such experiences (i.e. dependent upon mass media depictions alone) rate themselves as less vulnerable (Lavrakas, 1981; Perloff, 1984; Shotland et al, 1979).

Real-life experiences and TV influences. There is increasing research evidence that real life experiences of crime and law enforcement can make a difference to perceptions of television portrayals of crime and may affect relationships between exposure to televised crime and perceptions of crime in the real world. Elliott and Slater (1980) investigated relationships between viewing of law enforcement programmes and perceptions that various crime drama programmes were realistic. These relationships were examined for these different groups of adolescents – one group had had no direct experience with law enforcement agencies. Another group had had such contact in a positive way, through formal classes in law enforcement or sponsorship through school supplied by such agencies. A third group had had negative contact with law enforcement agencies because they had violated the law and been arrested, convicted and either incarcerated or put on probation.

It was found that students with positive law enforcement experience perceived crime drama programmes (eg *Charlie's Angels, Rockford Files, Hawaii Five-O*) in least realistic terms. The negative direct experience group on the other hand saw four out of six crime programmes as more realistic than either the limited or positive direct experience groups. The authors accept that their data cannot determine for sure whether heavier viewing levels contribute to more perceived realism or whether such programmes are watched because they are seen as realistic. Some sort of reciprocal relationship is likely.

In a subsequent study, the same authors again used these groups divided according to degree and nature of direct contact with law enforcement agencies as above (Slater and Elliott, 1982). Total television viewing and crime drama viewing were measured along with perceptions of the degree of realism for each of six law enforcement programmes on television at the time *(Baretta, Charlie's Angels, Hawaii Five-O, Rockford Files, Starsky and Hutch, Quincy)*. Then a number of questions were posed about societal safety, law enforcement processes and activity. In each of the latter cases, questions were posed and two possible answers were supplied – an accurate answer and an exaggerated answer – for respondents to choose from.

Multiple regression analyses revealed for the image of societal safety that negative direct experience, amount of law enforcement and perceived realism of law enforcement programmes were significant predictors. Young people whose experience with the police had resulted in some form of detention were less likely than the other students to see their environment as safe. Greater law enforcement viewing was associated with greater perceived safety, while greater perceived realism of law enforcement programmes predicted greater perceived danger. Understanding of law enforcement processes was positively associated with positive and negative direct experience with law enforcement and negatively with greater perceived realism of crime programmes. Negative direct experience and perceived programme realism were positively related to acceptance of television portrayals of police behaviour.

The evidence suggests that of the viewing/reality variables, the most important predictor variable is perceived law enforcement programme realism, a variable generally excluded from cultivation analysis studies. This variable consistently emerged as a significant predictor of social reality perceptions. It could be that if a programme is perceived as realistic, viewing it alone may be sufficient to influence social beliefs, quite apart from any or all other viewing. Gross viewing measures alone may therefore be wholly insufficient for the prediction of the nature of television cultivation effects.

Weaver and Wakshlag (1986) proposed that the direction and strength of the relationships between the amount of television viewed and perceptions of personal vulnerability to crime are contingent upon three factors: first, the viewer's predominant modality of criminal victimisation experience (direct, interpersonal or mediated); second, the types of television programmes viewed (crime-related or non-crime-related); and third, the contextual nature of the perceptions being considered.

Specifically, the influence of television's entertainment fare is "content specific" and, as a result, no significant relationships were expected between the amount of exposure to non-crime-related programmes and perceptions of personal vulnerability. but the viewer's reported exposure to crime-related programmes was expected to provide a differential pattern of significant relationships across the three modalities of criminal victimisation experience.

For those viewers who have no other source of information about criminal victimisation (mediated experience only), the exaggerated depictions of transgressive behaviour on television entertainment programmes would produce enhanced apprehension for personal safety, shaped by the television portrayals seen. Weaver and Wakshlag therefore looked for positive associations between amount of television crime-drama viewing and perceptions of personal vulnerability to crime.

Heavy exposure to crime-related television programmes following personal or interpersonal experience of violent crime might further enhance the viewer's perceptions of personal vulnerability. Gerbner et al (1980) refer to the concept of "resonance" in this context. It is possible though that heavy exposure to television entertainment programming might reduce anxieties (Zillmann, 1980). Zillmann (1982) acknowledged the violent crime shown on television, but noted that such programmes also typically feature the ultimate triumph of justice. He argued that television in fact distorts social "reality" in the other direction. By trivialising crime, repeated exposure diminishes the impact of previous experiences and alleviates the victim's worries.

In their investigation, Weaver and Wakshlag (1986) divided their respondents into three categories according to contact with crime. (1) Direct experience group composed of those who reported personal experience as a violent crime victim. (2) Interpersonal experience group, consisting of those who know someone who has been a victim. (3) Mediated experience group consisting of those with no direct or indirect contact as in the above two cases. They examined relationships between patterns of television viewing and crime-related anxieties. Through factor analysis, three anxiety categories were identified: situational, environmental and personal.

Situational anxieties referred to personal safety in "hypothetical" situations similar to the common theme of many crime-drama television programmes. For example, "You are home alone at night watching television. It is a pleasant evening and your windows are open. You hear some whispering voices outside, but you don't know exactly where they come from. How concerned would you be that you might be assaulted?"

Environmental anxieties refer to personal safety in respondents' residential locality. "How often do you decide not to walk alone at night because you are afraid of being the victim of a violent crime?"

Finally, personal anxieties refer to future personal involvement as the victim of a criminal act. "How likely is it that you personally will be a victim of some type of violent behaviour?" Relationships between these categories of perceptions and television viewing revealed content-specific associations. The number of non-crime-related programmes viewed which accounted for the bulk of prime-time viewing, was not related significantly to perceptions of personal vulnerability to crime either across the sample or within particular victimisation experience groups. On the other hand, crime viewing was related to apprehension within these groups.

For respondents who reported mediated experience, exclusively, crime-related viewing was related positively to concerns for personal safety in hypothetical situations similar to those typically depicted on TV drama and related weakly to more direct concerns for future personal victimisation. In the absence of other more direct sources of information, greater exposure to exaggerated depictions of crime on TV may tend to produce enhanced perceptions of likelihood of victimisation. However, the finding that the linkage is strongest at the non-personal level, but relatively weak at the personal level suggests that respondents may utilise intuitive knowledge about the veracity of fictional TV content when making crime-related judgements (Tyler, 1980; Wyer, 1980).

There was no evidence for the interpersonal group of "resonance". Knowing a victim of crime is not sufficient to amplify TV's impact on perceptions of personal vulnerability to crime – indeed knowing a victim may, suggest Weaver and Wakshlag, limit the impact of information concerning crime and violence conveyed by TV's entertainment form.

Among those individuals with direct experience of crime, there was a negative association between crime viewing and concerns for future personal involvement as a crime victim. This finding was consistent with the proposal that the selection of crime-related TV programmes – a relatively safe option even for a fearful person, may provide a means of relieving anomalies and apprehensions about future criminal victimisation. This is a theme we will return to in the last chapter.

Concluding remarks

In this chapter we have seen that the relationship between television viewing and beliefs about crime is not a simple one. The demonstration of a causal link between perceptions of crime and television viewing requires a sophisticated framework of analysis which takes into account several factors in addition to measures of how much television people say they watch and of their anxieties and beliefs about crime. How much television individuals watch in total may be less important than the extent to which they watch certain kinds of programmes with crime-related themes, and which therefore contain information of relevance to viewers' judgements and opinions about crime in real life. Even these more precise measures of what people watch on television may be insufficient on their own to produce accurate empirical statements about television's contribution to developing perceptions of crime. What may be more significant in this context are measures of how viewers perceive and interpret the content of television programmes. Are programmes with crime-related themes perceived to be realistic or as having any relevance to events in real life? If viewers dismiss programmes as irrelevant to their beliefs about the real world, the latter are unlikely to be influenced by television.

The extent to which television content is perceived to be relevant to the development of ideas about reality can vary, however, depending on the nature of those ideas. There is some indication that the media can have more influence on general beliefs about crime in society than on beliefs about one's own personal vulnerability to crime. Estimates of personal risk seem to be more sensitive to direct, personal experience of crime than to the secondary, vicarious experience provided by television and other mass media. The picture becomes further complicated by findings that perceived likelihood of involvement in crime, whether for self or others, and concern about personal victimisation, can vary across situations. Hence, even at a personal level, there may be certain special situations in connection with which concerns about crime may be influenced by relevant television content.

In conclusion, beliefs and concerns about crime are probably not influenced by television in an 'across-the-board' fashion. But there may be certain fairly specific relationships between perceptions of risk from certain types of crime in particular situations and exposure to informationally-relevant television crime content.

Chapter 6

Television and perceptions of crime: the British experience

Early British findings

Efforts to replicate Gerbner's findings among British samples in the late 1970s failed. Two studies, conducted by Piepe, Crouch and Emerson (1977) and by Wober (1978) tested relationships between levels of television viewing and personal fearfulness and interpersonal mistrust in the same manner as had been done previously by the Cultural Indicators research team at Philadelphia.

Piepe et al carried out 842 interviews in and around the Portsmouth area and related claimed amounts of television viewing to answers given to two wuestions: "These days a person doesn't know whom he can depend on", and "How often do you think that violent incidents happen around here?". For neither question did any substantial relationship emerge between claims of viewing and types of answers given.

The second survey, reported by Wober (1978), sampled over 1,000 adults over the age of 16 years throughout the United Kingdom. Again, respondents were posed two questions based on original items used by Gerbner and his colleagues, but worded in a slightly different way deemed to be more meaningful to British people. One of these items concerned the perception of how trustworthy people are and the other queried the perceived likelihood of being a victim of robbery. Together these items were combined to form a "security scale". Results indicated no systematic tendency for heavy viewers to have lower feelings-of-security scores than light viewers.

Several American writers subsequently challenged Wober's early find ings on methodological grounds. Neville (1980) argued that Gerbner's Cultural Indicators items and the reworded items from Gerbner forming Wober's "Security Scale" measure different attitude dimensions. However, this argument is countered by the results of a third British study which employed both re-worded items and others from Gerbner's scales in their original form and found that all these items loaded together on the same factor-analytic dimension (Wober and Gunter, 1982). The latter study will be examined in greater detail a little further on.

Another challenge to early British findings from across the Atlantic, designed to explain away the differences in American and British cultivation effects, was put forward by Hawkins and Pingree (1980). They argued that heavy viewers in Britain, at least based on the evidence of Wober (1978), probably see fewer violence-containing programmes per week than do viewers who watch equivalent amounts of television in the United States. Wober estimated that heavy viewers in Britain at the time of his 1978 study saw on average about ten and a half one-hour-long violence-containing programmes a week. Hawkins and Pingree estimate, on the other hand, from data provided in Gerbner's 1978 Violence Profile for US network prime-time television, that similar viewers in their own country would on average be likely to see more than twice that number of violent programmes each week.

In fact, on these estimates, the British *heavy* viewer may see less television violence than many American *light* viewers whose two hours or so of daily viewing may yield approximately twelve hours per week of programmes containing violence.

There are two questionable inferences assumed in this criticism however which throw doubt on its validity. First, in their cultivation analysis research in the late 1970s, Gerbner et al assumed a linear relationship between amount of viewing and levels of social anxiety and interpersonal mistrust – an assumption which has since been challenged following re-analysis of the same data base (Hirsch, 1980). Many of the survey samples studied by Gerbner were divided up into light, medium and heavy viewers according to different criteria of viewing (see Gerbner et al, 1977, 1978). This is a point which we shall return to in more detail further on in this chapter. Thus, relative differences in levels of viewing of British and American television audiences should not preclude the occurrence of similar patterns of differences in levels of anxiety and mistrust between lighter and heavier viewers in both societies.

Secondly, there is an erroneous comparison on which Hawkins and Pingree's criticism of this early British research was based which relates to implications about relative levels of violence-viewing among British and American TV audiences. These writers claim that British viewers probably see less TV violence than many American viewers. However, this assumption is based on measures of the relative occurrence of violence obtained by Gerbner's content analyses of prime-time TV programming only, whilst measures of levels of viewing amongst the public are based on all programmes, both within and outside peak-viewing times. The occurrence of violence in non-prime-time programming may be much less than that observed during prime-time, although Gerbner and his associates have obtained no data on this. Hence, American viewing figures cannot provide accurate indications of how much violent content the average viewer normally sees over the course of a week's viewing. Wober's study, however, based its viewing figures, not on amounts of TV watching in hours per day estimated by respondents themselves, but on actual programmes watched (obtained from diaries covering one whole week's TV output on all networks) which in turn are classifiable separately as violent or non-violent. Therefore, a much closer match can be expected here between the amount of time respondents spent watching television and the quantity of violent content they were exposed to during this time.

How else then might the discrepancies in British and American findings in the late 1970s be explained? One possible explanation could be that the cultivation effects of television interpreted by Gerbner et al in their secondary analysis of national public opinion survey data are specific to American audiences. If much peak-time programming in the two countries is of a similar range of types, however, this specificity of effect may be a function of US society itself or perhaps of the way television fits into that society rather than just of the nature of what is shown on television.

Another factor could be that the Cultural Indicators studies (e.g. Gerbner and Gross, 1976; Gerbner et al, 1977, 1978) have not generally taken into account the real levels of violence in different localities which might jointly determine views of the reality of social threat *and* the amount of viewing done if people decided to stay indoors to escape what they perceive as a frightening world outside. For example, in their Canadian study Doob and MacDonald (1979) reported that while people who watch a lot of television are more likely to indicate fear of their environment, this relationship disappears when the actual incidence of crime in the neighbourhood is taken into account. Their results implied that television viewing and people's fear of being victims of violence or crime may not be directly causally related.

Television and personal threat in Britain: later evidence

Wober and Gunter (1982) explored the possibility that relationships observed by previous authors between amount and type of television viewing and social anxiety, mistrust and alienation might be explained in terms of characteristics other than demographic ones which relate to individuals' personalities. The findings of Doob and MacDonald (1979) indicated that fear of environmental crime was related more closely to actual levels of such crime than to television watching. It is possible also amongst this Toronto population that in addition to making them more fearful high local crime rates encourage individuals to stay indoors and watch television.

This introduces another problem of how exactly the television viewing – social anxiety relationship is to be interpreted. The findings of all the major studies are essentially correlational and hence they cannot be used to infer direct causation. Therefore, whilst television viewing may indeed cultivate social fearfulness, it is equally reasonable to explain this relationship in terms of a reverse hypothesis, that it is those individuals who are more anxious to begin with who watch more television.

There is evidence from experimental studies conducted in the mid-1970s which indicates that mood states can affect the tendency to watch, and also may influence the specific type of content a person prefers to watch, Boyanowsky, Newtson and Walster (1974). In a later experiment Boyanowsky (1977) replicated and expanded his initial demonstration of this effect.

If transient mood states such as those studied by Boyanowsky can produce short-term film preferences, Wober and Gunter (1982)   argued that it is not unlikely nor unreasonable to assume that long-term viewing patterns may be influenced by permanent dispositions of individuals which relate not just to isolated environmental conditions or stimuli but to the prevailing social structure as a whole (see Srole, 1956; Merton, 1957). Rotter (1965) had developed an instrument designed to measure an enduring personality characteristic called *locus of control* which was supposedly shaped by the general and especially early experiences individuals had had with their social environment. What was more interesting about this measure was that the items used by Rotter were not dissimilar to those related to television viewing by Gerbner and his associates. The authors reasoned therefore that, rather than being a reaction simply to viewing large amounts of television drama as suggested by Gerbner *et al*, perception of social threat and danger may represent one aspect of a general system of beliefs associated with the underlying social reinforcement history of the individual. If this hypothesis is correct, then it was further reasoned that Rotter's measures of locus of control should correlate significantly with other measures of social anxiety and mistrust.

Whether or not it can be inferred that locus of control rather than television viewing underlies social anxiety depends on the demonstration of independent relationships of Rotter-type items and Gerbner-type items with viewing behaviour. A survey was therefore carried out amongst a sample of British viewers in London in which items (some reworded) from those used by Gerbner et al (1978, 1979) and others derived from

Rotter (1965) were used to test for variations in the degree of relatedness between amount of television viewing and perceptions of threat to personal security and of general mistrust and alienation.

Questionnaire-item responses were factor analysed and yielded four main factors which together accounted for 32 per cent of the common variance. Table 6.1 shows the factor loadings for each questionnaire item on these factors. Factor 1 was qualified by four items, including two Gerbner-type items on fear of victimization and thus was labelled *fear*.

Table 6.1. Factor loadings for opinion questionnaire items[a]

Factor name	Factors			
	1 Fear	2 Fate	3 Cynicism	4 Satis-faction
I am afraid to walk alone in my own neighbourhood at night (14)	*0.79*	0.15	0.11	−0.02
We live in a frightening world (15)	*0.62*	0.25	0.26	0.09
I worry about having my home burgled and property damaged (8)	*0.42*	0.21	0.20	−0.17
Most programmes are unsuitable for children (13)	*0.39*	0.18	0.33	−0.13
The pace of life is too much for me these days (3)	0.37	*0.60*	0.18	−0.08
Getting a good job depends mainly on being in the right place at the right time (11)	0.04	*0.48*	0.09	0.08
I feel that I have little influence over the things that happen to me (9)	0.27	*0.46*	0.21	−0.23
People's lives are controlled by accidental happenings (6)	0.07	*0.45*	0.12	0.04
Television news is the most reliable way to find out what is happening in the world (4)	0.14	*0.41*	−0.05	0.25
People are just out for what they can get these days (8)	0.14	0.07	*0.66*	−0.11
You've got to be pretty selfish these days (7)	0.14	0.07	*0.66*	−0.11
I am perfectly satisfied with my present standard of living (5)	0.05	-0.07	−0.01	*0.58*
Most people want to help you if you are in trouble (1)	0.00	0.09	−0.27	*0.50*
People are getting used to putting up with violence (2)	0.02	0.14	0.20	0.02
Family life is generally happier these days than it used to be (10)	0.02	−0.03	−0.08	0.13

[a]Varimax rotated factor matrix.
Note: Questionnaire item number given in parentheses.
Source: Wober and Gunter, 1982

Factor 2 was characterized by five items, including the three items from Rotter's locus of control scale and was termed *fate*. Factor 3 was defined by two items expressing feelings of selfishness or *cynicism* and factor 4 also consisted of two items which represented feelings of *satisfaction*.

Correlations were computed between these factors and viewing behaviour. These showed that amount of fiction viewing correlated significantly with the *fate* factor only, whilst amount of information viewing correlated significantly with all factors. At the same time correlations between factors themselves indicated that the Gerbner 'fear' factor and Rotter 'fate' factor were significantly correlated.

Viewing diaries which listed all programmes broadcast on the three major television channels during the week of the survey were used to measure amount of television viewing. Viewing was defined separately for two broad categories of programming – fiction and information. An initial series of correlations yielded a number of significant relationships between demographic variables (age and socio-economic class), and both opinions and television viewing. This left open the possibility that relationships between television viewing and social opinions were a function of third variables and had no independent association. Therefore, a series of partial correlations was computed to find out if the questionnaire factors had any residual relationship with viewing behaviours when the contribution of demographic variables was controlled. Analyses also looked at the effects of partialling out one factor on the strength of association between television viewing and the other factors. The results of these partial correlations are shown in Table 6.2.

Table 6.2. Partial correlations between social attitudes, demographic variables and TV viewing (n = 322)

Partial correlation between	Fear	Fate	Age	Class
Fate-fiction viewing	−0.23**	—	−0.25**	−0.22**
Fate-information viewing	−0.23**	—	−0.16*	−0.26**
Fear-fiction viewing	—	0.01	0.10	−0.08
Fear-information viewing	—	0.05	−0.06	−0.16*
Cynicism-fiction viewing	0.09	0.02	−0.11	−0.10
Cynicism-information viewing	0.10	0.04	−0.12	−0.14**
Satisfaction-fiction viewing	0.06	0.06	−0.11	0.05
Satisfaction-information viewing	−0.12	−0.12	0.06	−0.12
Age-fiction viewing	0.00	0.05	—	0.01
Age-information viewing	0.47**	0.45**	—	0.49**
Class-fiction viewing	0.14	0.10	0.16*	—
Class-information viewing	0.10	0.05	0.07	—

* P < 0.01
** P < 0.001
Source: Wober and Gunter, 1982

Wober and Gunter concluded that since the Rotter measure related significantly to the Gerbner factor while only the former was reliably associated with viewing behaviour in the presence of statistical controls for third variables, it could be that any relationships observed between fearfulness and television viewing may be little more than epiphenomena of deeper-seated personal dispositions or more general social conceptions, such as locus of control, which underlie both amount of viewing and the relatively superficial social perceptions tapped by fear of victimisation items.

As these findings are correlational, they can only be used to argue against the alleged source of distorted social perceptions, (that is, excessive television viewing) but not to establish another implied source of causation. This British evidence suggests, however, that whatever is measured by Gerbner's items is less robustly related to viewing behaviour than the factor measured by items derived from Rotter's scale (at least for viewers in Britain). Colloquially, it may not be television which makes viewers wary of the environment, but that people who are more fateful in their outlook on life generally stay in more to watch television and also express cautious attitudes.

The most recent British research has attempted to look in more detail at different levels of judgement about the prevalence of crime and of concerns about personal involvement, and how in each case they are related to viewing programmes with and without crime-related themes. Gunter and Wakshlag (1986) investigated the ways in which respondents' television viewing patterns (measured in terms of proportion of viewing time devoted to different categories of programming in addition to overall amount of viewing) were related to societal level and personal level judgements about crime in a variety of locations, urban and rural, both close to home and distant from it. We wanted to find out (a) whether societal level judgements were more closely related to television viewing than were personal level judgements; (b) whether perceptions of crime in some settings were especially closely related to television viewing; and (c) whether viewing of specific categories of programming, particularly those with crime-related content, predicted perceptions of crime better than did television viewing *per se*.

Television viewing diaries and attached questionnaires were sent to members of a London Panel maintained at the time of this research by the Independent Broadcasting Authority's Research Department for purpose of routine programme appreciation measurement. The diaries contained a complete list of all programmes broadcast on the four major television channels (BBC1, BBC2, ITV, Channel Four) in London during one week in February, 1985. Respondents assessed each programme seen on a six-point scale ranging from "extremely interesting and/or enjoyable" to "not at all interesting and/or enjoyable". Endorsements thus revealed not only appreciation levels, but also how many programmes had been seen, and of which kinds.

The questionnaire consisted of two parts. In the first part, respondents were asked about their personal experiences with crime and perceived competence to deal with an attack on themselves. More specifically, respondents were asked if they personally had ever been the victim of a violent crime, and if they knew anyone who had been. They were also asked to indicate along a five-point scale ranging from "strongly agree" to "strongly disagree" their extent of agreement with the statement "I could defend myself from an unarmed attacker". The latter item was presented with 11 items taken from or based upon Rubin and Peplau's (1976) Belief in a Just World scale. Some of these items were reworded in a more appropriate British idiom.

The second part of the questionnaire dealt with perceptions of the likelihood of crime and fears of personal victimisation, and was divided into three sections. In the first of these respondents were asked to estimate along a five-point scale (ranging from "not at all likely" [1] to "very likely" [5]) the probability that a person living in any of five locations would be assaulted in their lifetime (societal level judgements). The five locations given were London, Glasgow, Cotswolds, Los Angeles or on a farm in the United States. In the second section, estimates were requested from respondents concerning the likelihood that they might themselves fall victim to violent assault (personal level judgements) if they were to walk alone at night for a month around the area where they live, in a local park, through the streets of London's West End, through the streets of Glasgow, or through the streets of New York. They were also asked to say how likely they thought it was that they would become "the victim of some type of violent behaviour sometime in your lifetime" and that "you will have your home broken into during the next year".

In the final section, respondents were asked to say how concerned they would be for their personal safety (along a five-point scale ranging from "not at all concerned" [1] to "very concerned" [5]) if their car broke down at night in the English countryside, if they had to walk home alone late at night from a local pub, or if they found themselves having to walk through several streets in Los Angeles at night to reach their car.

A total of 448 usable diaries and attached questionnaires were returned giving a response rate of 47 percent. Data were then weighted to bring the sample in to line with population parameters.[1] With regard to television viewing behaviour, each respondent was given a score for the total number of programmes watched and the numbers watched for each of nine different categories of programmes: action-adventure, soap opera, British crime-drama, American crime-drama, films, light entertainment, sports, news and documentaries/general interest.

On the basis of a frequency distribution of the total number of programmes viewed during the survey week, respondents were divided into three categories by amount of viewing: light viewers (32 percent of the sample), medium viewers (34 percent) and heavy viewers (34 percent). Light viewers were those who watched fewer than 25 programmes during the week, which on the assumption of an average programme duration of half an hour, is equivalent to less than one and a half hours per day. Heavy viewers were those who watched more than 35 programmes a week (or more than three hours a day), and medium viewers were those who fell in between light and heavy viewing limits.

For each programme type, relative proportions of total viewing time devoted to each were computed by dividing the number of programmes seen in a category by the total number seen overall. This was done to obtain a more precise measure of how viewers shared out their total viewing time among different types of programmes. Frequency distributions were then computed on these viewing variables so that respondents could be divided into light, medium and heavy viewers within each programme category.

Experience with crime and competence to deal with it

Direct personal experience with violent crime was rare among this sample of London residents. Only seven percent of respondents said they had ever been the victim of a violent assault themselves. Indirect contact with violent assault through knowing someone else who had been a victim was more widespread; twenty-six percent said they knew a victim.

Further details are shown in Table 6.3, where a number of demographic differences in personal experience with violent crime can be discerned. Although men were only slightly more likely to say they had been victims themselves than were women, they were quite a lot more likely to know a victim. Age differences were apparent too. Younger people (aged under 35 years) were nearly twice as likely as older people to say they had been

[1]Demographic characteristics of the sample								
	Sex		Age			Class		
Total	Males	Females	16-34	35-54	55+	ABC1	C2	DE
n 448	218	230	183	139	126	211	130	106
% 100	49(48)	51(52)	41(36)	31(34)	28(28)	47(47)	29(26)	24(28)

Percentage figures in parentheses represent the known proportions for each demographic category in the London ITV region based on Broadcasters' Audience Research Board (BARB) Establishment Survey figures for 1985.

victims of an assault. Indeed, nearly one in ten young people said they had had this experience.

Knowing a victim was equally likely across age-bands however. Directly experienced personal victimisation was more commonplace among working class (DE) respondents than among middle class (ABC1) respondents.

Respondents had mixed opinions about whether they could effectively defend themselves against an unarmed attacker. Responses were equally divided between those who judged that they could defend themselves (32 percent), those who thought they could not (34 percent) and those who were unsure either way (34 percent).

Once again, as Table 6.3 illustrates, there were marked differences of opinions among individuals associated most strongly with sex and age. Men were nearly three times as likely as women to have confidence in their ability to look after themselves, while younger and middle-aged respondents had greater confidence than did older respondents.

Table 6.3. Personal experience and competence to deal with violent assault upon oneself

	Sex			Age			Class		
	All %	Male %	Female %	16-34 %	35-54 %	55+ %	ABC1 %	C2 %	DE %
Have you ever been the victim of a violent crime?									
Yes	7	8	6	9	7	4	6	5	10
No	93	92	94	91	92	96	94	95	90
Has anyone you know ever been the victim of a violent crime									
Yes	26	31	21	24	33	25	28	22	25
No	73	69	79	76	67	75	72	78	75
I could defend myself from an unarmed attacker									
Agree	32	49	17	39	34	22	35	32	31
Disagree	34	19	47	26	29	48	32	35	35
Unsure	34	32	36	34	37	30	34	34	35

Perceived likelihood of victimisation: others

Respondents were asked to estimate the likelihood that a person living in each of five different locations would become a victim of a violent assault during their lifetime. Results indicated that greatest risk was perceived to exist for people living in urban locations. Such locations in the United States, however, held a great deal more danger than their equivalents in Britain. As Table 6.4 shows, the place seen as potentially the most dangerous to live in by Londoners was Los Angeles. Far fewer respondents perceived similar likelihood of a person being a victim of assault in Glasgow and central London. The locations perceived as safest of all were rural areas, both in Britain and the United States.

Women were more likely than men to perceive victimisation as a likely occurrence for others across four out of the five locations. There was also a marked class differential, particularly with respect to perceptions of risk in the West End of London. Working-class respondents were much more likely to perceive social danger for others.

Table 6.4. Perceived likelihood of victimisation for others during their lifetime*

	Sex			Age			Class		
	All	Male	Female	16-34	35-54	55+	ABC1	C2	DE
Likelihood of being assaulted for a person living in:									
Los Angeles	77	72	81	77	76	77	74	78	81
Glasgow	49	44	55	46	47	56	48	48	54
London (West End)	43	38	46	46	32	49	36	41	56
Farm in USA	11	7	15	13	13	8	10	9	15
Cotswolds	3	3	3	3	4	2	1	2	7

* Percentages are of those who, on a five-point risk scale, scored likelihood of assault as either 4 or 5.

Perceived likelihood of victimisation: self

How much danger did respondents perceive in the world for themselves? Results once again showed that perceived likelihood of victimisation varied across different locations. The scenarios painted for respondents in this section of the questionnaire once again varied along one dimension in particular – their degree of proximity to where they lived. As Table 6.5 shows, perceived danger levels rose with increasing distance from home. Far and away the most dangerous place to walk alone at night, for this London sample, was New York. New York was perceived to hold real risks of personal assault for more than five times as many respondents as was their own neighbourhood. Few respondents perceived any real danger in their own neighbourhood.

Table 6.5. Perceived likelihood of victimisation for self.*

	Sex			Age			Class		
	All %	Male %	Female %	16-34 %	35-54 %	55+ %	ABC1 %	C2 %	DE %
Likelihood of being assaulted oneself if walking after dark alone in:									
New York	83	70	87	85	81	84	84	81	87
Glasgow	53	45	59	46	55	57	49	58	52
London (West End)	41	33	53	47	38	44	33	50	57
Local Park	30	23	42	35	27	37	25	37	44
Own neighbourhood	15	10	19	12	11	20	12	13	21
Likelihood of being a victim in own lifetime	21	24	17	25	16	20	20	23	18
Likelihood of having home burgled in next year	23	23	27	20	22	36	22	26	30

* Percentages are those who, on a five-point risk scale, scored likelihood of assault or
personal risk as either 4 or 5.

There were demographic differences in levels of perceived risk to
personal safety. Across all locations, women more often perceived a
strong likelihood of being violently assaulted than did men. The gap
between the sexes was smallest with regard to perceived danger in the
local neighbourhood, where it was reduced to nine percent. Age was not
as consistently associated with differences in perceptions of danger to
self across locations. The most marked difference emerged with respect
to perceptions of risk in one's own locality, where older people more
often thought they were likely to become victims than did younger or
middle-aged people. Class was associated with risk perceptions for self,
but only with respect to more proximal locations for respondents. Thus
working class respondents were more likely than middle-class respondents to mention the possibility of danger to self from violence in central
London, a local park and in their own neighbourhood. However, working
class respondents did not think of themselves as likely to fall victim to
any violence in their lifetime more often than middle class respondents.

Fear of victimisation

How afraid were respondents of being victims of violence? To what extent did concern for personal safety vary with the location in which one might find oneself? Three items were presented dealing with fear of victimisation. Results presented in Table 6.6 indicate that respondents said they would be most concerned for their personal safety if they found themselves walking alone after dark in the streets of Los Angeles. Fear of being assaulted was mentioned twice as often for Los Angeles as in either of two British locations. Respondents associated the least amount of fear with being stranded after dark in the English countryside.

Table 6.6. Fear of victimisation.*

	Sex			Age			Class		
	All %	**Male** %	**Female** %	**16-34** %	**35-54** %	**55+** %	**ABC1** %	**C2** %	**DE** %
Fearful of walking alone after dark in Los Angeles	87	61	81	67	67	84	69	69	81
Fearful of walking alone after dark from local pub	47	30	64	41	45	60	42	44	65
Fearful of being stranded in English countryside after dark	27	13	41	24	24	35	23	26	38

* Percentages of those who, on a five-point scale of concern for personal safety, scored either 4 or 5.

Demographic differences emerged associated with sex, age and class of respondents. Fear of personal victimisation was most often mentioned across all locations by women, the elderly and working-class respondents. Differences between the responses of men and women, the young and old, middle-class and working-class were quite substantial in every case.

Personal experience with violence and risk perceptions

To what extent do direct and indirect real life experiences with violence and belief in one's own ability to defend oneself against an assailant colour or mediate perceptions of social danger?

As the results presented in Table 6.7 indicate, whether or not respondents had ever been victims of violence themselves or knew someone who had been, made little difference to their perceptions of the likelihood of others being victimised. Belief about one's competence to defend oneself, however, did make a difference. With respect to risk perceptions for people living in urban locations in particular, whether in Britain or the USA, respondents who felt incapable of defending themselves effectively were more likely to perceive danger.

Table 6.7. Personal experience and competence to deal with violence and perceptions of likelihood of assault for others.

	Whether been a victim		Whether know a victim		Competence to defend oneself	
	Yes %	No %	Yes %	No %	High %	Low %
Likelihood of being assaulted for a person living in:						
Los Angeles	75	77	81	77	63	76
Glasgow	53	50	55	48	40	54
London (West End)	44	42	44	42	38	50
Farm in USA	8	11	12	5	11	15
Cotswolds	2	3	4	3	4	4

One might expect personal experiences with violence to have a more substantial impact on perceived environmental risks to oneself than in relation to perceptions of risk for others. The results, however, as shown in Table 6.8, indicate otherwise. For most scenarios neither direct nor indirect experience with violence oneself differentiated risk perceptions relating to self. The one notable exception was for perceived chance of being assaulted in one's own neighbourhood. Respondents who had been victims of an assault before were more likely than those who had not to perceive danger near to home.

Once again, though, belief in one's own ability to handle trouble emerged as an important mediator of risk perceptions. Across all locations, local and distant, perceived likelihood of personal victimisation was greater among respondents who had little confidence in their ability to defend themselves.

Two more estimates of personal risk exhibited stronger associations with personal experiences with violence however. Victims of violence were three times as likely as others to say they thought they would be victims of criminal assault during their lifetime. Clearly, and not surprisingly, the experience of victims had coloured their outlook. Indirect contact with violence, through knowing a victim, proved less powerful as a discriminator of perceptions. And so too did belief in one's competence to defend oneself. Perceived likelihood of having one's home broken into was related in the opposite direction to the above perception to personal experience with violence. Victims were *less* likely to believe there was a good chance of being burgled during the next year. Perceived risk from burglary was predictably (given the above findings) greater among respondents lacking confidence in their ability to defend themselves.

Table 6.8. Personal experience and competence to deal with violence and perceptions of likelihood of assault for self

	Whether been a victim		Whether know a victim		Competence to defend oneself	
	Yes %	**No** %	**Yes** %	**No** %	**High** %	**Low** %
Likelihood of being assaulted oneself if walking after dark alone in:						
New York	85	85	88	84	73	85
Glasgow	49	53	58	51	40	61
London (West End)	49	42	38	45	36	53
Local Park	30	34	29	34	24	47
Own neighbourhood	24	14	12	16	5	26
Likelihood of being a victim in own lifetime	56	18	25	19	21	27
Likelihood of having home burgled in next year	17	26	26	24	21	33

Personal experience with violence and fear of victimisation

As Table 6.9 shows, respondents who had had previous experience of being victims of a violent assault were in general more concerned for their safety within each of the scenarios that had been painted for them. This factor made the most profound difference with respect to the most local of the three settings – the scenario in which respondents had to imagine themselves walking home alone late at night from a local pub.

Indirect experience was a less powerful discriminator, although it did make some difference with respect to British scenarios. In contrast to direct experience, however, indirect experience with violence was associated with being less fearful.

The most powerfully related variable of all was belief in one's self defence competence. For judgements of concern for personal safety in settings at home and abroad, respondents who felt they could not effectively defend themselves against an unarmed attacker were more concerned about their chances of being assaulted.

Table 6.9. Personal experience and competence to deal with violence and fear of victimisation.

	Whether been a victim		Whether know a victim		Competence to defend oneself	
	Yes %	No %	Yes %	No %	High %	Low %
Fearful of walking alone after dark in Los Angeles	79	71	70	72	54	79
Fearful of walking alone after dark from local pub	60	46	41	50	31	73
Fearful of being stranded in English countryside after dark	33	26	20	30	18	46

Television viewing and perceptions and fear of victimisation

The results above indicate marked variations in some perceptions of victimisation associated with certain demographic characteristics of respondents, their direct and indirect experience of assault and perceived self-defence capability. In order to find out if television viewing or viewing of specific programme types were related to risk perceptions independently of these other variables, a series of multiple regression analyses was run in which ten television viewing variables, demographics, personal experience with violence (direct and indirect), belief in ability for self-defence, and belief in a just world, were related to each risk perception. Each regression procedure was executed with all independent variables entered equally.

Table 6.10 shows the results for perceptions of risk for others. As this table shows, in the presence of multiple statistical controls for other variables, there was only one instance of a television viewing variable exhibiting a significant relationship with a victimisation-likelihood perception.

Viewing of television news was negatively related to perceived likelihood of victimisation for someone who lives in Los Angeles.

Heavier viewing of the news predicted the perception of less danger in Los Angeles for others. None of the serious drama or crime-related programme categories (e.g., action-adventure, US crime-drama, UK crime-drama) was significantly related to any perceptions of risk for others.

Table 6.10. Multiple regressions showing relationships between television viewing, personal experience with violence and demographics with perceived likelihood of victimisation for others

	\. London		Risk for person who lives in: Los Angeles		Glasgow		Cotswolds		Farm in USA	
	Beta	t	Beta	t	Beta	t	Beta	t	Beta	t
Total TV										
viewing	.06	1.00	.02	.33	-01	-25	.00	.07	.02	.26
Action										
adventure	.11	1.43	-07	-87	.02	.31	-03	.43	-02	-30
Soap operas	.05	.87	.10	1.69	.01	.25	.06	1.06	.03	.51
Sport	-0.44	-.77	-04	-83	-05	-91	-09	-173	-01	.14
Light										
entertainment	-04	-78	-09	-1.53 *	.04	.73	-05	-84	-10	-1.80
News	-04	-64	-13	-2.05	-06	-99	.00	.02	-03	-45
Documentaries	-05	-89	-02	-35	-03	-63	-04	-82	-01	-19
Films	-03	-49	-05	.78	-10	-1.54	.02	.30	-01	-20
US crime drama	-001	.10	.14	1.93	-00	.06	-01	.10	.13	1.82
UK crime drama	.02	.28	-08	-1.49	.04	.68	-03	-60	-09	1.58 *
Sex	.09	1.68	.09	1.66	.07	1.38	-00	-02	.11	2.09
Age	-00	-01	.00	.05	.10	1.92	-06	-1.02	-05	-88
Class	.14	2.84 **	.05	1.00	.07	1.28	.13	2.57	.06	1.22
Just world	-07	-1.44	-01	.16	.05	-1.09	-01	.27	.02	.41
Been a victim	-03	-50	-04	-79	-06	-1.12	-01	.27	.02	.41
Know a				**		**				*
victim	-07	-1.25	-16	-3.09	-15	-2.16	-01	-20	-12	-2.17
Defend oneself	.07	1.40	.06	1.04	.04	.80	.09	1.61	.06	1.13
Multiple R	.30		.31		.27		.23		.27	
Multiple R²	.09		.10		.07		.05		.07	
F	2.33		2.46		1.89		1.26		1.79	
df	17/399		17/392		17/398		17/399		17/390	
P	.002		.001		.02		ns		.03	

Levels of statistical significance: *** P < 0.001, ** P < 0.01, * P < 0.05

More significantly to these perceptions were whether respondents knew a victim of an assault. Respondents who knew a victim perceived greater danger for others who live in Los Angeles, Glasgow and rural USA.

Table 6.11 presents the results for similar analyses computed for perceptions of likely risk to self in different locations. Six significant relationships emerged between these perceptions and television viewing variables. Viewing of soap operas and of UK crime-drama predicted perceived risk in own neighbourhood. Heavier viewing of both programme types predicted the perception of greater danger to self in this setting. Total television viewing was significantly related to perception of potential danger in a local park and in London's West End at night. In both instances, heavier viewing predicted perception of greater risk. Finally, soap operas emerged as significant predictor of perceived personal danger if walking alone at night in the streets of New York and perceived likelihood of having one's home burgled in the next year. Heavier soap opera viewing predicted greater perceived danger in New York, but less perceived danger of being burgled.

Self-defence capability emerged most consistently as a significant predictor of perceived likelihood of self-victimisation across settings. Greater confidence is being able to defend oneself was associated with a reduction in perceived likelihood of being assaulted.

Table 6.12 presents the results for fear of victimisation. Heavier total television viewing was a significant predictor of level of concern in all three scenarios. Throughout, heavier television viewing predicted greater concern for personal safety. With regard to the scenario closest to home, (i.e., walking home alone at night from a local pub) concern for safety was also predicted by amount of viewing of action-adventure, US crime-drama and sport. Heavier viewing of each of these programme categories predicted greater concern for personal safety.

In summary, this survey among London residents which investigated their perceptions of crime at home and abroad, found that perceived likelihood of victimisation for others and for self, and concern about victimisation for self, varied with the situation, demographic characteristics of respondents, their direct experience with crime, and confidence in personal ability for self-defence in the face of an assault. Television viewing patterns, however, were relatively weak and inconsistent indicators of judgements about crime.

Unlike the findings of Tyler (1980, Tyler and Cook, 1984), no evidence emerged here that societal level judgements (e.g., perceived risks for others) were more strongly linked to media experiences than were personal level judgements about crime (e.g., perceived risk for self). If anything, television viewing variables were more often and more powerfully related to perceptions of risk for self. One note of consistency

Table 6.11. Multiple regressions showing relationships between television viewing, personal experience with violence and demographics with perceived likelihood of victimisation for self

Own area	Local park		London west end		New York		Glasgow		Victim lifetime		Home burgled			
	Beta	t	Beta	t	Beta	t	Beta	t	Beta	t	Beta	t	Beta	t
Total TV viewing	.01	.19	.13	2.33*	.14	2.55**	.08	1.41	.06	1.08	.06	.95	.08	1.36
Action adventure	.05	.67	.04	.51	.02	.29	.01	.14	-01	-09	.08	1.07	.14	1.81*
Soap operas	.12	2.10*	.06	1.16	.05	.82	.15	2.70**	.08	1.38	-01	-25	-13	-2.21*
Sport	-05	-97	-08	-1.68	-10	-1.92	-02	-45	-07	-1.38	-05	-86	-08	-1.49
Light entertainment	-11	-1.97	-04	-74	-05	-90	-03	-51	.04	.76	-06	-99	-03	-54
News	-02	-33	.04	.76	-04	-72	-02	-30	-04	-59	-07	-1.19	-01	-20
Documentaries	-07	-1.23	-03	-61	-02	-46	-00	-04	-06	-1.15	-04	-77	-03	-49
Films	-09	-1.41	-07	-1.18	-06	-94	06	.92	-05	-84	-00	-01	-03	-54
US crime	-08	-1.19	-01	-10	-00	-04	-00	.01	-05	-73	-07	-1.03	-08	-1.08
UK crime	.11	2.07*	.04	.83	02	.30	-04	-75	.05	.96	.01	.23	03	.62
Sex	.05	1.03	.20	3.89**	.10	1.90*	.11	2.07	.02	.31	-07	-1.37	-03	-48
Age	.03	.55	-00	.04	-06	-113	-08	-1.40	.07	1.28	-05	-99	.11	2.03*
Class	.10	2.08*	.13	2.69**	.22	4.37***	.04	.82	.04	.72	.00	.07	.07	1.41
Just world	-.06	-1.23	-02	-41	-05	-1.04	.04	.76	-09	-1.77*	-12	2.48*	-07	-1.37
Been a victim	-02	-41	-04	-82	03	.63	-01	-28	.06	1.19	-19	-3.59***	.00	.08
Know a victim	.04	.85	.01	.20	-02	-32	-17	-3.19**	-12	-2.23*	.00	.08	.04	.68
Defend oneself	.15	2.83**	.13	2.62**	-09	1.65	03	.53	.13	2.50**	.03	.54	.11	1.97*
Multiple R	.33		.41		.37		.30		.30		.29		.25	
Multiple R²	.11		.17		.14		.09		.09		.09		.06	
F	2.87		4.79		3.78		2.23		2.27		2.19		1.53	
df	17/399		17/399		17/399		17/392		17/396		17/399		17/397	
P	.0001		.0001		.0001		.004		.003		.004		.08	

Levels of statistical significance: *** p < 0.001, ** P < 0.01, * P < 0.05

Table 6.12. Multiple regressions showing relationships between television viewing, personal experience with violence and demographics with fear of victimization.

	Concern if:					
	Stranded English countryside		At night in Los Angeles		Walk home at night from pub	
	Beta	t	Beta	t	Beta	t
Total TV viewing	.11	2.09 *	.13	2.23 *	.13	2.51 **
Action adventure	.12	1.70	.00	.09	.14	4.02 **
Soap operas	.05	.97	.10	1.74	.08	1.52
Sport	-06	-1.20	-09	-1.65	-15	-3.15 **
Light entertainment	-01	.18	-06	-1.13	-03	-57
News	.00	.07	-06	-96	.04	-73
Documentaries	-07	-1.51	-07	-1.28	-04	-73
Films	-03	-54	.02	.75	-06	-1.09
US crime drama	-11	-1.72	-02	-35	16	2.45 **
UK crime drama	.03	.58	.01	-15	.00	.03
Sex	.31	6.42 ***	.15	2.88 **	.28	5.89 ***
Age	.03	.67	.08	1.46	.08	1.60
Class	.14	3.11 **	.09	1.76	.15	2.23 **
Just world	-02	-37	-10	-2.02 *	-00	-04
Been a victim	-05	-97	-06	-1.24	-09	-2.02 *
Know a victim	.06	1.24	-03	-51	.06	1.34
Defend oneself	.15	3.14 **	.08	1.53	.12	2.50 **
Multiple R	.51		.39		.54	
Multiple R²	.26		.15		.29	
F	8.35		3.90		9.22	
df	17/398		17/379		17/387	
P	.0001		.0001		.0001	

Levels of statistical significance: *** P < 0.001, ** P < 0.01, * P < 0.05

with Tyler, however, was the fact that personal experience with crime was an important predictor of personal level likelihood judgements and fear of crime.

At the personal level, victimisation perceptions varied with the situation. Respondents were less likely to perceive danger close to home than in more distant situations. Furthermore, in the case of one variable, self-defence capability, its significance as a predictor seemed to depend upon the situation about which judgements were being made. Thus, lacking confidence in one's ability to defend oneself predicted the perception of greater danger to self and greater concern for safety, but only in British locations. There was no such obvious patterning to television viewing predictors of victimisation perceptions across different situations however.

Five television viewing variables emerged from the regression analyses as significantly related to perceptions of likelihood of self-victimisation and fear of victimisation. These were total amount of television viewing, soap opera viewing, sport, UK crime drama-viewing and US crime drama-viewing. The last three, however, were significantly related only to one perception in each case.

Perceived likelihood of self victimisation in one's own neighbourhood was greater among heavier than among lighter viewers of soap operas and UK crime-drama. Greater potential danger to self in a local park in London's West End at night was connected with heavier viewing of television in general. Heavier soap opera viewing meanwhile predicted greater perceived likelihood of personal attack at night in New York, but lower perceived likelihood of being burgled.

With regard to concern about being a victim of assault, however, there was some indication that television viewing was a better predictor in the context of situations closer to home. Greater fear of victimisation across all three situations was linked to heavier total television viewing. In the situation that was probably closest (geographically) to home for respondents in this survey, however, fear of victimisation when walking home alone late at night from a local pub was also predicted by heavier viewing of action-adventure, sport and US crime drama.

Researchers previously have noted the importance of content specificity in the relationship between television viewing and perceptions of crime (Weaver and Wakshlag, 1986). From this observation, one would expect crime perceptions to be predicted best of all by levels of exposure to programmes with crime-related content, such as action-adventure and crime drama. Evidence for this sort of linkage emerged sporadically in this study. Heavier UK crime drama viewing was associated with greater perceived likelihood of self-victimisation in one's own neighbourhood. Heavier viewing of action-adventure and US crime drama was linked with greater concern about personal safety if walking home from a local pub alone late at night.

In the context of personal-level likelihood-of-victimisation beliefs, the best programme category predictor was soap operas. Heavier viewing of soap operas predicted greater perceived danger in one's own area and in New York, but less chance of being burgled. These findings are not entirely inconsistent with the notion of content-specificity as a mediator of television's influence in social reality perceptions, however. It has been noted by several US researchers, for example, that crime had been a major theme in soap operas for a long time (Katzman, 1972; Cassata, Skill and Boadu, 1979) and that it is becoming a more prominent focus in these programmes (Sutherland and Siniawsky, 1982; Estep and Macdonald, 1985).

With respect to fear of crime, viewing of particular categories of programmes seemed to be less relevant than simply how much television is consumed overall. This may indicate that if television is the causal agent, it really does not matter which programmes individuals watch. Rather, it is general levels of exposure that are most significant. Alternatively, it could be that television is the affected agent, with viewing levels being influenced among other things by the fearfulness of individuals. Those who have greater anxieties about possible dangers to self in the social environment may be driven to spend more time indoors watching the box. Probably nearest to the truth though may be a notion of circularity in the relationship. Greater fear of potential danger in the social environment may encourage people to stay indoors, where they watch more television, and are exposed to programmes which tell them things which in turn reinforce their anxieties.

Chapter 7

Television influences in perspective

Crime surveys have revealed that people have certain ideas about their personal likelihood of involvement in crime. However, people have been found often to overestimate the risks to themselves and others compared with what actual statistical probabilities would indicate. At another level, people may also be fearful of crime. But fears vary from one type of person to the next, and in regard to different sorts of crime (Hough and Mayhew, 1985). Personal concern about crime is not invariably associated with perceptions about likelihood of personal risk. In other words, someone may believe that the chances of their becoming a victim of crime are remote, but are nevertheless anxious about the possibility that it might happen. Thus, likelihood perceptions and fear are conceptually distinct (Zillmann and Wakshlag, 1985).

According to some experts, distorted perceptions and heightened anxieties about crime may derive from exaggerated stories about crime in the media. The media often give prominent coverage to certain types of violent crimes which may produce inflated public estimates about the frequency of what are in actuality the least frequent sorts of crimes (Conklin, 1975). Reliance on the media for information about crime may mean that many people have few other sources against which to compare the veracity of media-accounts. Under such circumstances, some theorists believe that the media can exert powerful conditioning effects on public beliefs.

A major body of research in the United States has investigated relationships between the public's use of television and their perceptions and fear of crime (Gerbner and Gross, 1976; Gerbner et al, 1977, 1978, 1979). The results of this investigation have been interpreted by its authors to show that there is a link between television viewing and what people believe about the real world. People who watch television frequently tend to perceive real-life crime as more commonplace than do people who are less frequent viewers.

The conclusion that this finding demonstrates an effect of television, however, has been challenged on the ground that the research on which it is based has not always taken sufficiently into account the influences of other important factors. Characteristics of individuals such as their age, sex, social class, level of education, area of residence and psychological dispositions have been found to underlie both how much they watch television and their beliefs about crime (Doob and Macdonald, 1979; Hughes, 1980; Wober and Gunter, 1982). When these other variables are controlled, relationships between television viewing and perceptions of crime have often been found to weaken considerably or to disappear altogether.

The challenge based on controls for "third variables" is not without its pitfalls though. One reason for this is that television viewing may be related to social beliefs in different ways among different demographic groups. Thus, simple statistical controls for these variables may produce an artificial reduction in the link between viewing behaviour and perceptions of social reality (Gerbner et al 1980b). This counter-argument is valid to a point, but it cannot account for other weaknesses inherent in the basic framework of analysis, which includes only measures of overall amount of television viewing and undifferentiated perceptions of crime.

There are now firm indications that the demonstration of an influence of television on perceptions and fears of crime requires a much more sophisticated framework of analysis. The total amount of television people claim to watch, for instance, may often be less important to anxieties or beliefs about crime than the particular programmes they watch. Judgements about real-life crime may be influenced more by reality programmes than by fictional programmes (Tamborini et al, 1984). In addition, it is important to take into account viewers' perceptions of the content of programmes they watch. Programmes may be differentiated by broadcasters into reality and fictional types, but are these programmes perceived by the viewers to be differentially realistic? Research has shown that viewers are capable of making highly refined judgements about television violence (Gunter, 1985; van der Voort, 1986). The same applies to judgements about television portrayals of criminals and law enforcers (Rarick et al, 1973). The extent to which television is perceived to be realistic can limit the influences it has on viewers' beliefs (Potter, 1986). If programmes are categorised as being divorced from reality and therefore as containing no information relevant to everyday life, they are unlikely to have much influence on what viewers think about the world around them.

Whether television content has any effect on beliefs about crime, however, can also depend on the nature of those beliefs. Individuals may hold beliefs about the incidence of crime in society at large which are distinguishable from beliefs they hold about personal risks of victimisation. Research indicates that personal-level judgements tend to be affected mostly by direct experience of crime and not to any great extent by the media. In contrast, societal-level beliefs about crime tend to be more sensitive to information received about crime through the media (O'Keefe, 1984; Tyler, 1980; Tyler and Rasinski, 1984). In the absence of more direct sources of information, crime content on television may affect perceptions of likelihood of victimisation at a societal level, but still hardly at all at a personal level (Weaver and Wakshlag, 1986).

A further level of complexity is introduced into the equation by the finding that perceived likelihood of falling victim to crime, for self and others, and fear of personal victimisation, can very across situations (Gunter and Wakshlag, 1986). People tend generally to perceive greater risk of victimisation both for themselves and for others in urban locations than in rural locations, and in locations that are geographically some distance away from where they live than in locations closer to home. The analyses presented in earlier chapters do not exhaust all the possibilities regarding different types of situations important to perceptions of crime. It could be, for instance, that even locations close to home are perceived to be dangerous if local experience has taught people that that is the way things are. Also there may be occasions when locations which are geographically not very far away, are nevertheless completely unfamiliar to individuals on the basis of first-hand experience. People who live in the suburbs of a big city, for example, may rarely venture into some central zones which they know, either through word of mouth or media reports, to be dangerous, crime-ridden places. The important point is that perceptions and fears of crime are often situation-specific, and are not influenced in a generalised way by television. There may, however, be certain specific relationships between perceptions of risk from crime in particular situations and viewing of particular programmes or programme types which contain information relevant to those perceptions. But even when such fairly specific associations between television exposure and perceptions of crime have been demonstrated, the case for television as the causal agent is still not proven.

Turning cultivation around

Several writers have observed that a key problem with the cultivation hypothesis lies in its reliance on correlational evidence to make causal statements about the relationships of television viewing and its cultivation effects (Wober and Gunter, 1982; Zillmann, 1980). It is not just that the evidence presented by the Cultural Indicators research team frequently failed to take adequate account of third variables when interpreting their significant correlations between weight of viewing and social perceptions, but more critically, in a conceptual as well as methodological sense, their model has failed to determine in what direction the relationship lies.

In determining whether television violence causes fearfulness and anxiety about crime in viewers, or whether anxiety fosters heavy viewing, Zillmann (1980) argues for the latter alternative. While acknowledging that the display of transgression is an essential part of drama, he notes that such fare also.typically features the ultimate triumph of justice. The criminal is caught, and the forces of law and order prevail. Zillmann argues that suspenseful drama on television may distort realities but proposes that the bias is more likely to be in the direction of presenting an overly just, overly safe world. If the portrayal of criminal acts adversely affects the viewer's perceptions of reality, the anxious viewer should find comfort and relief in drama that presents the triumph of the "forces of good". Anxious people may resort to watching such action-adventure drama because it ultimately *reduces* their anxieties by projecting a just world, an image that may occur on television far more frequently than in their real life experiences. Is there any evidence to support this selective viewing hypothesis?

In a survey with a national sample in the USA, Mendelsohn (1983) reported a number of interesting relationships between the need to know about the prevention of crime and extent to which people watched crime dramas or paid attention to crime news. This study provides evidence not only for a selectivity hypothesis but also for cultivation of a different kind of effect from those emphasised by the Annenberg group.

Concerns about potential victimisation often associated with residing in a dangerous neighbourhood were positively related to attention to news about crime in all major media and extent of viewing crime-drama programmes on television. In relation especially to viewing televised crime fiction, Mendelsohn found that frequent viewers are likelier to believe they have a great deal of control over things that affect their personal lives, are more apt to believe that individual citizens can do things to help reduce crime, and are more often highly confident tabout their own ability to protect themselves against crime. Mendelsohn's findings indicate that individuals who say they have a need for information about protection from crime turn to certain kinds of media content (eg, crime-drama programmes) in order to learn, if at all possible, strategies for crime prevention. Mendelsohn concludes that these programmes may therefore serve a valuable instrumental function for certain kinds of people living in threatening environments, and, if "the media cultivate anything they appear to cultivate crime prevention competence among such publics – not hysteria" (Mendelsohn, 1983, p.7).

Despite frequent criticism of the nature of crime-related entertainment programming on television, O'Keefe (1984) reported no connections between how much people reported watching such programmes and their perceptions and attitudes regarding crime in the real world. The only assumption was a tendency among viewers of those programmes to regard crime more often as an inevitable social ill.

The statistical relationship between claims of watching news about crime on television and audience perceptions of crime signifies a potential television influence that appears to be somewhat more problematic. It is difficult to disentangle the direction in which this relationship operates from correlational information about their association above. Does watching crime news cause greater concern about crime among viewers, or do people who are already more concerned about crime selectively attend more to such news?

In all probability the answer is neither one nor the other, but instead there may be some form of reciprocal or mutually reinforcing interaction between television and audience predispositions. People who are already more concerned about crime watch news about crime in order to get more information about the issue or to have their existing suppositions confirmed.

It is not only news about crime which apprehensive people may turn to, however, but also fictional content with crime themes. Doob and MacDonald (1979), for example, found that individuals who lived in high crime areas, who were thus more fearful of crime, not only watched more television, but also spent a larger proportion of their viewing time with crime drama shows. Thus, more apprehensive individuals, living in high crime neighbourhoods, appear to be selectively watching crime drama. This assumption was corroborated by earlier research findings. Boyanowsky, Newtson and Walster (1974) observed that threatened individuals exhibited a distinct preference for viewing potentially fear-inducing events under safe conditions. After a much publicised brutal murder of a freshman coed at the University of Wisconsin, attendance at a movie shown locally that featured psychopathic killings ("In Cold Blood") greatly *increased* relative to a another comparison movie. Girls who had shared a dormitory with the murder victim showed greater preference subsequent to the murder for the murder movie than for a non-violent romantic film, whereas girls from another dormitory, who were presumably less directly affected by the murder, showed no such preference. Despite the likelihood that the murder film might have reinstated salient anxieties, female students did not avoid it.

Subsequently, Boyanowsky (1977) found that threating conditions, which ostensibly evoke fear or apprehension, enhanced preferences for exciting media content, including some which depicted violence. In a controlled experiment on the effects of acute fear of victimisation, a deception was played on female students who were led to believe that a girl had just been attacked either nearby on their own university campus (a condition of high threat) or on another campus across town (low threat). The information was provided by a uniformed campus guard who also told them to be especially alert and careful when walking home after the experiment in which they were to take part and which was run at night. Women in a control condition were supplied with no such threatening information.

In what to the students appeared to be the experiment, the girls were given a choice among various films they could watch, and they rated the desirability of viewing these films. The materials, described in synopsis, were: (a) a romantic comedy, (b) a romantic interlude, (c) an instructional film about women's self-defence against men, (d) a drama featuring male violence toward females, (e) a drama featuring anti-male violence, and (f) a sex orgy.

The apprehension treatment had no appreciable affect on the desirability of seeing any of the first four offerings. Although the self-defence information was useful under the circumstances, fearful females showed no greater appetite for it than did their more relaxed counterparts. Also the fearful women did not display any higher desire for the film that promised the victimisation of women by men. The last two choices were significantly affected by apprehension, however. Compared with the control, the desirability of seeing anti-male violence tripled in both threat conditions and the eagerness to watch an orgy doubled. According to Zillmann and Wakshlag (1985), one explanation for these results is that females who are anxious about a rapist on the loose locally may enjoy watching a movie featuring violence between men, because it shows some men being victimised. And anxious females may be attracted to sexual themes because men making love are rendered innocuous. However, in the final event, Zillmann and Wakshlag admit that the findings are difficult to explain.

Another study by Bryant et al (1981), which was discussed in Chapter Five, also included assessment of selective exposure. Beginning one week or so after the conclusion of a week on a special viewing diet during which its immediate effects on perceptions of crime had been measured, further measures were taken. First, subjects were encouraged to watch more television dramas as part of a class assignment. Several tapes were made available in the library and consumption was unobtrusively recorded. Second, subjects were instructed to keep a television viewing diary over a four-week period. Then a marketing firm approached them and offered payment if they would keep diaries for a further three weeks – a request to which many responded.

Results indicated that subjects who had been fed a heavy diet of television drama featuring justice restoration were likely to exhibit increased viewing of crime drama, whereas heavy prior viewing of drama depicting injustice in its resolution produced less crime drama viewing. The use of drama tapes on reserve at the library revealed this pattern, as did viewing diaries. However, for instructor solicited diaries, the consumption – depressing effect of drama depicting injustice fell short of significance, and for the commercially solicited diaries, the consumption – enhancing effect of drama dwelling on justice fell short.

Zillmann and Wakshlag (1985) suggest that individuals who were heavily dosed with crime-drama depicting restoration of justice found such programmes satisfying and developed a taste for them. On the other hand, those shown a heavy diet of crime-drama in which justice does not prevail found this sort of programme less than satisfying, not to their tastes, (perhaps even disturbing) and were turned off to television crime drama.

The strongest evidence yet for an influence of crime apprehension on selective viewing of crime drama has come from a study by Wakshlag, Vial and Tamborini (1983). In an experimental investigation, Wakshlag et al (1983) manipulated individuals' initial apprehension levels before giving them the opportunity to select films to be viewed from a list. Participants in this study were shown either a documentary about crime or an innocuous documentary about the Himalayas. A series of items designed to measure degree of apprehension about crime or fear of victimisation were given after viewing and indicated that the crime documentary did produce significantly stronger apprehension reactions. Participants were then shown a list of titles of films with accompanying synopses which, according to earlier independent evaluations, varied in the degree to which they featured victimisation and restoration of justice. Individuals who saw the crime documentary chose fewer victimisation and more justice restoration films than did their counterparts who saw the nature films.

Strong sex differences also emerged. Violence in drama appealed to males much more than to females. Regardless of these sex differences, however, the appeal of violence in television drama dropped significantly for individuals who were apprehensive about the possibility of being victimised themselves. This finding indicates that violence *per se* is not an attractive element of entertainment for people who are fearful of victimisation. For such individuals, violence is a turn-off.

Looking at the effect of restoration of justice, it emerged that this held more appeal to females than to males. Crime apprehensive individuals established great sensitivity to the theme of justice restoration. The appeal of drama featuring this theme grew significantly with such apprehensions. Hence, people who are worried about crime may seek comfort in programmes in which justice is restored or prevails.

In another experimental study, Wakshlag, Bart, Dudley, Groth, McCutcheon and Rolla (1983) explored the mechanics of excitement and enjoyment of crime drama by people apprehensive about crime. Individuals who had low and high apprehension about crime (assessed by earlier data) were assigned to conditions in which they saw an excerpt from a crime drama programme in which either the protagonist or the antagonist was ultimately killed.

Physiological measures taken during viewing indicated that apprehensive people responded more strongly to victimisation in drama than did non-apprehensive people. Apprehensive individuals, for instance, exhibited greater increases in heart rate and blood pressure readings during exposure. This difference in response was specific to crime drama. Evaluations of the programmes' endings were also different in the two apprehension groups. Apprehensive individuals tended to be more disturbed by the violent endings, and they consequently tended to enjoy them less than did their less apprehensive counterparts.

Although dramatic storylines in fictional television programmes often feature violent conflict between the good guys and the bad guys, giving the impression of a violent world infiltrated by criminal activity, nearly all such programmes finish on the note of good triumphing over evil, and with the ultimate bringing to justice of law-breakers. If television has a lesson to teach about the world, it is equally or more likely to be that the world is a just and safe place than that it is a dangerous one (Zillmann, 1980).

In a survey which both tested this hypothesis and examined the possibility that beliefs may determine viewing patterns and preferences rather than the other way around, Gunter and Wober (1983) posted viewing diaries and opinion questionnaires to a representative London panel from whom 500 usable replies were returned. The diaries indicated how much television and what types of programmes respondents watched during they survey week. The questionnaire contained items of personal fearfulness, interpersonal mistrust, anomie and belief in a just world. The latter were from a scale developed by Rubin and Peplau (1975) to measure the extent to which people believe the world is a just place. This dimension is regarded, much as locus of control had been, as an enduring characteristic that can reliably discriminate between individuals.

Respondents' scores on each of the above social belief dimensions were related to the overall amount of television viewing and amount of viewing specific categories of programming such as action-adventure, soap operas, news and current affairs, and US television series. Results showed that in the presence of multiple statistical controls for sex, age and social class, just two significant relationships survived between viewing behaviour and social beliefs.

Respondents who had strong just-world beliefs tended to be heavy viewers of action-adventure programmes and US television series (which consisted mainly of action-adventure anyway). These relationships suggest a cultivation effect of television which runs in opposition to that proposed and observed by Gerbner and his colleagues. Among the British viewers sampled in this survey, the social message assimilated from action drama programmes related to the triumph of justice over evil rather than the harm that criminals are frequently shown to inflict on innocent or law-abiding others. It could also be said, however, that these results do not reflect a cultivation effect of television at all, but instead indicate that people who believe that the world is a just place selectively watch dramatic content to obtain reinforcement and clarification of their beliefs.

References

Arons, S. and Katsch, K. (1977) How TV cops flout the law. *Saturday Review* (March), 11-19.

Bandura, A. (1973) *Aggression: A social learning analysis.* Englewood Cliffs, N.J.: Prentice-Hall.

Bandura, A. (1977) *Social leaning theory.* Englewood Cliffs, N.J.: Prentice-Hall.

BBC (1972) *Violence on Television : Programme content and viewer perceptions.* London: British Broadcasting Corporation.

Bell, D. (1962) *The end of ideology.* New York: Free Press

Berkowitz, L. (1970) The contagion of violence: An S-R mediational analysis of some effects of observed aggression. In W. J. Arnold and M.M. Page (Eds.) *Nebraska Symposium on Motivation,* Lincoln, NE.: University of Nebraska Press.

Blumer, H., and Hauser, P.M. (1933) *Movies, delinquency, and crime.* New York : The Macmillan Company

Bouwman, L. (1970) Cultivation analysis: The Dutch case. In G. Melischek, K.E. Rosengren and J. Stappers (Eds.), *Cultural indicators: An international symposium.* Vienna, Austria, Austrian Academy of Sciences.

Bouwman, H. and Stappers, J. (1984) The Dutch violence profile: A replication of Gerbner's message system analysis. In G. Melischek, K.E. Rosengren and J. Stappers (Eds.), *Cultural indicators : An international symposium.* Vienna, Austria: Austrian Academy of Sciences.

Boyanowsky, E.O. (1977) Film preferences under conditions of threat: Whetting the appetite for violence, information or excitement? *Communication Research, 4,* 33-145.

Boyanowsky, E.O., Newtson, D. and Walster, E. (1974) Film preferences following a murder. *Communication Research, 1,* 32-43.

Bryant, J., Carveth, R.A. and Brown, D. (1981) Television viewing and anxiety: An experimental examination. *Journal of Communication, 31,* 106-119.

Cassata, M. B., Skill, T.D. and Boadu, S.O. (1979) In sickness and in health. *Journal of Communication, 29,* 73-80.

Clark, D.G. and Blankenberg, W.B. (1972) Trends in violent content in selected mass media. In G. Comstock and E. Rubinstein (Eds.) *Television and social behaviour, Vol. 1, Media content and control.* Washington, D.C.: U.S. Government Printing Office.

Collins, W. A. (1973) Effect of temporal separation between motivation, aggression and consequences: A developmental study. *Developmental Psychology, 8,* 215-221.

Collins, W. A. (1979) Children's comprehension of television content. In E. Wartella (Ed.), *Children communicating: Media and development of thought, speech, understanding.* Beverly Hills, CA: Sage, pp. 21-52.

Collins, W.A. (1981) Recent advances in research on cognitive processing of television viewing. *Journal of Broadcasting, 25,* 327-334.

Conklin, J.E. (1971). Dimensions of community response to the crime problem. *Social Problems, 18* (Winter), 373-385.

Conklin, J.E. (1975). *The impact of crime* New York: Macmillan

Cook, F.J. (1971) There's always a crime wave. In D.R. Cressey (Ed.), *Crime and criminal justice.* Chicago: Quadrangle Books.

Dale, E. (1935) *The content of motion pictures* New York: The Macmillan Company

De Fleur, M. L. (1964) Occupation roles as portrayed on television. *Public Opinion Quarterly, 28,* 57-74.

De Fleur, M.L. and De Fleur, L.B. (1967) The relative contribution of television as a learning source for children's occupational knowledge, *American Sociological Review, 32,* 777-789.

Doob, A.N. and Macdonald, G.E. (1979) Television viewing and fear of victimisation : Is the relationship causal? *Journal of Personality and Social Psychology, 37,* 170-179.

Dominick, J.R. (1973) Crime and law enforcement in prime-time television. *Public Opinion Quarterly, 37,* 243-250.

Drabman, R.S. and Thomas, M.H. (1974) Does media violence increase children's toleration of real-life aggression? *Developmental Psychology, 10,* 418-421.

Dysinger, W.S., and Ruckmick, C.A. (1933) *The emotional responses of children to the motion picture situation* New York: The Macmillan Company

Elliott, W.R. and Slater, D. (1980) Exposure, experience and perceived TV reality for adolescents. *Journalism Quarterly, 57,* 409-414.

Estep, R. and Macdonald, P.T. (1985) Crime in the afternoon : Murder and robbery on soap operas. *Journal of Broadcasting and Electronic Media, 29,* 323-331.

Fazio, R. H. and Zanna, M. P. (1981) Direct experience and attitude-behaviour consistency. In L. Berkowitz (Ed.), *Advances in experimental social psychology* (Vol. 14, pp. 161 – 202). New York: Academic Press.

Friedman, K., Bischoff, H., Davis, R. and Person, A. (1982) *Victim and helpers : Reactions to crime.* Washington, DC: National Institute of Justice.

Garofalo, J. and Laub J. (1978, 1981) The fear of crime: broadcasting our perspective. *Victimology: An International Journal, 3,* 242-253.

Gerbner, G. (1972) Violence in television drama : Trends and symbolic functions. In G.A. Comstock and E. Rubinstein (Eds.), *Television and social behaviour, Vol 1, Media content and control.* Washington, D.C. : U.S. Government Printing Office. pp. 28-187.

Gerbner, G. and Gross, L. (1976) Living with television : The violence profile. *Journal of Communication, 26,* 173-199.

Gerbner, G., Gross, L., Eleey., Jackson-Beeck, M., Jeffries-Fox, S. and Signorielli, N. (1977) Television violence profile no. 8 : The highlights. *Journal of Communication, 27,* 171-180.

Gerbner, G., Gross,L., Jackson-Beeck, M., Jeffries-Fox, S. and Signorielli, N. (1978) Cultural indicators : Violence profile no. 9 *Journal of Communication 28,* 176-207.

Gerbner, G., Gross, L., Signorielli, N., Morgan, M. and Jackson-Beeck, M. (1979) The demonstration of power: Violence profile no. 10. *Journal of Communication, 29,* 177-196.

Gerbner, G., Gross, L., Morgan, M. and Signorielli, N. (1980a) Some additional comments on cultivation analysis. *Public Opinion Quarterly, 44,* 408-410.

Gerbner, G., Gross, L., Morgan, M. and Signorielli, N. (1980b) The 'mainstreaming' of America : Violence profile No.11 *Journal of Communication, 30,* 10-29.

Gerbner, G., Gross, L., Morgan, M. and Signorielli, N. (1981a) A curious journey into the Scary World of Paul Hirsch. *Communication Research, 8,* 39-72.

Gerbner, G., Gross, L., Morgan, M. and Signorielli, N. (1981b) Final reply to Hirsch. *Communication Research, 8,* 259-280.

Gordon, M. and Heath, L. (1981) The news business, crime and fear. In D. Lewis (Ed), *Reactions to crime,* Beverly Hills, CA: Sage.

Graber, D B.(1980) *Crime news and the public.* New York: Praeger.

Gross, L. and Morgan, M. (1985) Television and enculturation. In J.R. Dominick and J. E. Fletcher (Eds), *Broadcasting research methods.* Boston: Allyn and Bacon, Inc.

Gunter, B. (1985) *Dimensions of television violence.* Aldershot, England: Gower Publishing Company.

Gunter, B. and Wober, M. (1983) Television viewing and public trust. *British Journal of Social Psychology, 22,* 174-176.

Gunter, B. and Furnham, A. (1984) Perceptions of television violence: Effects of programme genre and physical form of violence. *British Journal of Social Psychology, 23,* 155-184.

Gunter, B. and Furnham, A. (1985) Androgyny and perceptions of male and female violence on television. *Human factors, 38,* 353-359.

Gunter, B. and Wakshlag, J. (1986) *Television viewing and perceptions of crime among London residents.* Presented at the International Television Studies Conference, Institute of Education, London, July 10 – 13.

Halloran, J. D. and Croll, P. (1972) Television programmes in Great Britain. In G. A. Comstock and E. A. Rubinstein (Eds.) *Television and Social Behaviour, Vol. 1, Content and Control.* Washington, D. C.: U.S. Government Printing Office, pp. 415-492.

Hawkins, R. and Pingree, S. (1980) Some progress in the cultivation effect. *Communciation Research, 7,* 193-226.

Hawkins, R. and Pingree, S. (1982) Television's influence on social reality. In D. Pearl, L. Bouthilet, and J, Lazar (Eds.), *Television and behaviour: Ten years of scientific progress and implications for the eighties.* (DHSS Publication No. ADM 82-1196, Vol 2, pp. 224-247). Washington, DC: US Government Printing Office.

Heath, L. (1984) The impact of newspaper crime reports on fear of crime: A multi-methodological investigation. *Journal of Personality and Social Psychology, 47,* 263-276.

Hedinsson, E. (1981) *TV, family and society : The social origins and effects of adolescents' TV use.* Stockholm, Sweden : Almqvist & Wiksell, International.

Hedinsson, E. and Windahl, S. (1984) Cultivation analysis: A Swedish illustration. In G. Melischek, K. E. Rosengren and J. Stappers (Eds.) *Cultural indicators: An international symposium.* Vienna, Austria: Austrian Academy of Sciences.

Himmelweit, H.T., Swift, B. and Biberian, M.J. (1978) The audience as critic: An approach to the study of entertainment. In P. H. Tannenbaum (Ed.) *The entertainment functions of television.* New York : Lawrence Erlbaum Associates.

Hirsch, P. (1980) The 'scary' world of the non-viewer and other anomalies : A reanalysis of Gerbner et al's findings on cultivation analysis: Part I. *Communication Research, 7,* 403-456.

Hough, M. and Mayhew, P. (1985). *Taking account of crime: key findings from the 1984 British Crime Survey.* London: Her majesty's Stationery Office.

Howitt, D. and Cumberbatch, G. (1974) Audience perceptions of violent television content. *Communication Research. 1,* 204-223.

Hughes, M. (1980) The fruits of cultivation analysis : A re-examination of the effects of television in fear of victimisation, alienation and approval of violence. *Public Opinion Quarterly, 44,* 287-302.

Issacs, N.E. (1961) The crime of crime reporting. *Crime and delinquency, 7* (October), 313-320

Katzman, N. (1972) Television soap operas : What's been going on anyway? *Public Opinion Quarterly, 36,* 200-212.

Krugman, H.E. and Hartley, E.L. (1970) Passive learning from television. *Public Opinion Quarterly, 34,* 184-190.

Lavrakas, P. (1980) On households. In D. Lewis (Ed), *Reactions to crime : Individual and institutional responses.* (pp. 67-85) Beverly Hills, CA: Sage.

Leyens, J-P., Parke, R.D., Camino, L. and Berkowitz, L. (1975) Effects of movie violence on aggression in a field setting as a function of group dominance and cohesion. *Journal of Personality and Social Psychology, 32,* 346-360.

Lichter, S. and Lichter, R. (1983) *Prime time crime.* Washington, DC: The Media Institute.

Liebert, R. M. and Baron, R.A. (1972) Some immediate affects of televised violence on children's behaviour. *Developmental Psychology, 6,* 469-475.

Melischek, G., Rosengren, K.E. and Stappers, J. (1984) *Cultural indicators: An international symposium.* Vienna, Austria: Austrian Academy of Sciences.

Mendelsohn, H. (1983) *Using the mass media for crime prevention.* Paper presented at the annual convention of the American Association for Public Opinion Research, Buck Hill Falls, PA, May, 1983.

Merton, R.K. (1957) *Social theory and social structure.* Glencoe, IL: Free Press.

Morgan, M. (1984) Symbolic victimization and real world fear. In G. Melischek, K.E. Rosengren and J. Stappers (Eds.), *Cultural indicators: An international symposium.* Vienna, Austria : Austrian Academy of Sciences. (pp.365-387).

Neville, T. (1980) *Television viewing and the expression interpersonal mistrust.* Unpublished doctoral dissertation, Princeton University.

O'Keefe, G.J. (1984) Public views on crime : Television exposure and media credibility. In R, N. Bostrom (Ed.), *Communication Yearbook, 8.* Beverly Hills, CA : Sage, pp.514-535.

Parke, R.S., Berkowitz, L., Leyens, J-P, West, S.G. and Sebastian, R.J. (1977) Some effects of violent and non-violent movies on the behaviour of juvenile delinquents. In L. Berkowitz (Ed.), *Advances in experimental social psychology,* vol 10., New York : Academic Press.

Packer, H. (1968) *The limits of criminal sanctions.* Stanford, C. A.: Stanford University Press.

Perloff, L.S. (1984) *The effect of indirect experience on perceived vulnerability to victimization.* Paper presented to the meeting of the Midwestern Psychological Association, Chicago, May, 1984.

Piepe, A., Crouch, J. and Emerson, M. (1977) Violence and television. *New Society, 41,* 536-538.

Pingree, S. (1983) Children's cognitive processing in constructing social reality. *Journalism Quarterly, 60,* 415-422.

Pingree, S. and Hawkins, R. (1981) US programmes on Australian television : The cultivation effect. *Journal of Communication, 31,* 97-105.

Potter, W.J. (1986) Perceived reality and the cultivation hypothesis. *Journal of Broadcasting and Electronic Media, 30,* 159-174.

Quinney, R. (1970) *The social reality of crime.* Boston: Little, Brown

Rarick, D. L., Townsend, J. E. and Boyd, D. A. (1973) Adolescent perceptions of police: Actual and as depicted in TV drama. *Journalism Quarterly, 50,* 438-446.

Reeves, B., Chaffee, S.H. and Tims, A. (1982) Social cognition and mass communication research. In M.E. Roloff and C.R. Berger (Eds.), *Social cognition and communication.* (pp 287-326). Beverly Hills, CA : Sage.

Reyes, R.M., Thompson, W.C. and Bower, G.H. (1979) Judgemental biases resulting from differing availabilities of arguments. *Journal of Personality and Social Psychology, 37,* 357-368.

Rosenberg, M. (1957) *Occupation and values.* Glensoe, IL : Free Press.

Rotter, J.B. (1965) General expectancies for internal versus external control of reinforcement. *Psychological Monographs, 80,* (1, Whole No. 609).

Schramm, W., Lyle, J. and Parker, E.B. (1961) *Television in the lives of our children.* Stanford : Stanford University Press.

Shotland, R. L., Hayward, S. C., Young, C., Signorella, M. L., Mindingal, L. K., Kennedy, J.K., Rovine, M.J. and Danowitz, E.F. (1979) Fear of crime in residential communities. *Criminology, 17,* 34-57.

Signorielli, N. (1984) The demography of the television world. In G. Melischek, K. E. Rosengren and J. Stappers (Eds.), *Cultural Indicators: An international symposium.* Vienna, Austria: Austrian Academy of Sciences.

Singer, J. L. (1980) The power and limitations of television: A cognitive-affective analysis. In P.H. Tannenbaum (Ed.) *The entertainment functions of television.* Hillsdale, N.J. : Lawrence Erlbaum Associates.

Skogan, W.G. and Maxfield, M.G. (1981) *Coping with crime.* Beverly Hills, CA: Sage.

Slater, D. and Elliott, W. R. (1982) Television's influence on social reality. *Quarterly Journal of Speech, 68,* 69-79.

Smythe, D.W. (1954) *Three years of New York Television : 1951 – 1953.* Urbana, Il: National Association of Education Broadcasters.

Srole, L. (1956) Social interpretation and certain corollaries. *American Sociological Review, 21,* 709-716.

Srull, T.K. and Wyer, R.S. (1979) The role of category accessibility in the interpretation of information about persons : Some determinants and implications. *Journal of Personality and Social Psychology, 37,* 1660-1672.

Suedfeld, P., Little, B.R., Rauch, A.D., Rawle, D.S. and Ballard, E.S. (1985) Television and adults : Thinking, personality and attitudes. In T.M. Williams (Ed.), *The impact of television,* New York: Academic Press.

Sutherland, J.C. and Siniawsky, S.J. (1982) The treatment and resolution of moral violation on soap operas. *Journal of Communication, 32,* 67-74.

Tamborini, R., Zillmann, D. and Bryant, J. (1984) Fear and victimisation: Exposure to television and perceptions of crime and fear. In R.N. Bostrum (Ed.), *Communication Yearbook 8,* (pp. 492-513) Beverley Hills, CA: Sage.

Tannenbaum, P. H. (1979) TV images of the police: Docu-drama production. *In Annual Review of Audience Research Findings,* London: British Broadcasting Corporation.

Tannenbaum, P.H. and Zillmann, D. (1975) Emotional arousal in the faciliation of aggression through communcation. In L. Berkowitz (Ed.), *Advances in experimental social psychology,* vol 8, New York: Academic Press.

Tate, E.D. (1976) *Viewer perceptions of selected television shows.* The Royal Commission on Violence in the Communications Industry, Research Report, Ontario, Canada.

Teevan, J. J. and Hartnagel, T. F. (1976) The effect of television violence on the perception of crime by adolescents. *Sociology and Social Research, 60,* 337-348.

Tyler, T.R. (1980) The impact of directly and indirectly experienced events: The origain of crime-related judgements and behaviours. *Journal of Personality and Social Psychology, 39,* 13-28.

Tyler, T.R. (1984) Assessing the risk of crime victimisation and socially-transmitted information. *Journal of Social Issues, 40,* 27-38.

Tyler, T.R. and Cook, F.L. (1984) The mass media and judgements of risk: Distinguishing impact on personal and societal level judgements. *Journal of Personality and Social Psychology, 47,* 693-708.

Tyler, T.R. and Rasinski, K. (1984) Comparing psychological images of the social perceiver: Role of perceived informativeness, memorability and effect in mediating the impact of criminal victimisation. *Journal of Personality and Social Psychology, 46,* 308-329.

Van der Voort, T. H. A. (1986) *Television violence : A child's eye view.* Amsterdam: Elsevier Science Publishing Company, Inc.

Wakshlag, J., Bart, L., Dudley, J., Groth, G., McCutcheon, J. and Rolla, C. (1983) Viewer apprehension about victimisation and crime drama programmes. *Communication Research, 10,* 195-217.

Wakshlag, J., Vial, V. and Tamborini, R. (1983) Selecting crime drama and apprehension about crime. *Human Communication Research, 10,* 227-242.

Weaver, J. and Wakshlag, J. (1986) Perceived vulnerability to crime, criminal victimisation experience, and television viewing. *Journal of Broadcasting and Electronic Media, 30,* 141-158.

Wober, M. (1978) Televised violence and paranoid perception : The view from Great Britain. *Public Opinion Quarterly, 42,* 315-321.

Wober, M. and Gunter, B. (1982) Television and personal threat: Fact or artifact? A British view. *British Journal of Social Psychology, 21,* 43-51.

Wyer, R.S. and Srull, T.K. (1980) Category accessibility : Some theoretical and empirical issues concerning the processing of social stimulus information. In E.T. Higgins, C.P. Herman, and M.P. Zanna (Eds), *Social cognition: The Ontario Symposium of personality and social psychology,* Hillsdale, N.J. : Lawrence Erlbaum Associates. pp. 161-197.

Zillmann, D. (1979) *Hostility and aggression.* Hillsdale, N.J. : Lawrence Erlbaum Associates.

Zillmann, D. (1980) Anatomy of suspense. In P.H. Tannenbaum (Eds) *The entertainment functions of television.* Hillsdale, N.J. : Lawrence Erlbaum Associates.

Zillmann, D. and Wakshlag, J. (1985) Fear of victimization and the appeal of crime drama. In D Zillmann and J Bryant (Eds), *Selective exposure to communication.* Hillsdale, N.J. : Lawrence Erlbaum Associates.